White Horse Inn

A Musical Comedy

Eric Maschwitz, Bernard Grun,
Hans Müller, Erik Charell and
Harry Graham

A Samuel French Acting Edition

SAMUELFRENCH-LONDON.CO.UK
SAMUELFRENCH.COM

Copyright © 1933 by Coliseum Syndicate D.23509
Copyright © 1957 (Acting Edition) by Samuel French Ltd
All Rights Reserved

WHITE HORSE INN is fully protected under the copyright laws of the British Commonwealth, including Canada, the United States of America, and all other countries of the Copyright Union. All rights, including professional and amateur stage productions, recitation, lecturing, public reading, motion picture, radio broadcasting, television and the rights of translation into foreign languages are strictly reserved.

ISBN 978-0-573-08034-0

www.samuelfrench-london.co.uk

www.samuelfrench.com

FOR AMATEUR PRODUCTION ENQUIRIES

UNITED KINGDOM AND WORLD EXCLUDING NORTH AMERICA

plays@SamuelFrench-London.co.uk

020 7255 4302/01

Each title is subject to availability from Samuel French, depending upon country of performance.

CAUTION: Professional and amateur producers are hereby warned that WHITE HORSE INN is subject to a licensing fee. Publication of this play does not imply availability for performance. Both amateurs and professionals considering a production are strongly advised to apply to the appropriate agent before starting rehearsals, advertising, or booking a theatre. A licensing fee must be paid whether the title is presented for charity or gain and whether or not admission is charged.

The professional rights in this play are controlled by Eric Glass Ltd, 25 Ladbroke Crescent, London W11 1PS.

No one shall make any changes in this title for the purpose of production. No part of this book may be reproduced, stored in a retrieval system, or transmitted in any form, by any means, now known or yet to be invented, including mechanical, electronic, photocopying, recording, videotaping, or otherwise, without the prior written permission of the publisher. No one shall upload this title, or part of this title, to any social media websites.

The right of Eric Maschwitz, Bernard Grun, Hans Müller, Erik Charell and Harry Graham to be identified as author of this work has been asserted by them in accordance with Section 77 of the Copyright, Designs and Patents Act 1988

WHITE HORSE INN
CHARACTERS
(in the order of their appearance)

KATHI, the Postwoman
KARL, "piccolo" waiter at the *White Horse Inn*
A FORESTER
ZENZI, a goatherd
A COURIER
FRANZ, a waiter
LEOPOLD, head waiter at the *White Horse Inn*
JOSEPHA VOGELHUBER, owner of the *White Horse Inn*
THE STEAMER CAPTAIN
BRIDEGROOM
BRIDE
JOHN EBENEZER GRINKLE, a manufacturer
OTTOLINE, his daughter
VALENTINE SUTTON, a solicitor
SIGISMUND SMITH, another manufacturer
PROFESSOR HINZEL, a professor
GRETEL, his daughter
THE MAYOR
THE MAYOR'S LADY SECRETARY
THE EMPEROR
KETTERL, his servant
LANDLORD of *The Travellers' Rest*

VILLAGERS, CHAMBERMAIDS, TOURISTS, WAITERS, WAITRESSES, ALPINE GUIDES, SAILORS, TRAVELLERS, DAIRYMAIDS, FARMHANDS, MARKET-WOMEN, COUNCILLORS, POLICE, TEACHERS, FIREMEN, BANDSMEN, A.D.C.s, GAMEKEEPERS, CLIMBERS

SYNOPSIS OF SCENES

ACT I
SCENE 1 Outside the *White Horse Inn*
SCENE 2 The Cow-shed
SCENE 3 Outside the Inn

ACT II
SCENE 1 Outside the Inn
SCENE 2 The Pine Wood
SCENE 3 The Town Hall
SCENE 4 The Cow-shed
SCENE 5 Outside the Inn

ACT III
SCENE 1 Outside the Inn
SCENE 2 *The Travellers' Rest*
SCENE 3 Outside the Inn

Time—Prior to 1914

KEY TO PRONUNCIATION

KATHI — Kárt-ti
ZENZI — Zent-zi
LEOPOLD — Láy-o-pold
JOSEPHA — Yo-záy-fa
SIGISMUND — Síg-is-mund
SALZKAMMERGUT — Sáltz-kammer-goot
ISCHL — Ísh-ul
MALCHEN — Márl-shen
PUPPERL — Póop-erl
GURKENSALAT — Góor-ken-sal-árt
EDELWEISS — Aídle-vice
MADERL — Máy-durl
FAHRKARTE — Fár-carter

MUSIC

ACT I

	Overture	
No. 1	Introduction	Kathi, Quartet and Chorus
No. 1a	Reprise	Zenzi
No. 2	Entrance of Tourists	Leopold and Chorus
No. 3	"It Would Be Wonderful"	Josepha, Leopold and Girls
No. 4	Arrival of the Guests	Chorus
No. 5	"The White Horse Inn"	Sutton, Josepha, Chorus and Dancers
No. 5a	Exit music	
No. 5b	Melos	
No. 6	"Happy Cows"	Dairymaids and Dancers
No. 7	"Your Eyes"	Sutton, Ottoline, Chorus and Dancers
No. 8	Finale Act I	Leopold and Chorus

ACT II

No. 9	Entr'acte and Opening Chorus	Josepha, Leopold and Market-women
No. 10	"Good-bye"	Leopold and Men
No. 10a	Exit music	
No. 11	"You, too"	Sutton, Ottoline and Dancers
No. 11a	Exit music	
No. 12	"In Salzkammergut"	Josepha, Grinkle, Chorus and Dancers
No. 12a	Melos	
No. 13	"Sigismund"	Sigismund, Chorus and Dancers
No. 13a	Dance	Sigismund and Gretel
No. 14	Ballet. "Salzkammergut"	Sutton, Grinkle, Kathi, Chorus and Dancers
No. 15	"Fairies"	Sigismund and Gretel
No. 15a	Change of scene music	
No. 15b	Fight music	
No. 15c	Change of scene music	
No. 16	Finale Act II	Leopold, Josepha, Sutton and Chorus

▼

ACT III

No. 17	Entr'acte and Serenade	Chorus
No. 18	Recitation	Emperor
No. 18a	Reprise	Sutton, Ottoline and Josepha
No. 18b	Dance	Male Dancers
No. 19	"My Song of Love"	Ottoline, Sutton, Chorus and Dancers
No. 19a	Exit music	
No. 19b	Reprise	Gretel and Sigismund
No. 20	Finale Act III	Ensemble
No. 20a	Finale Ultimo	Ensemble
No. 20b	**Play-out music**	

ADAPTORS' NOTE

White Horse Inn was first produced in Britain at the London Coliseum on the 8th April 1931. As directed by Erik Charell, its spectacular beauty and melodious score took London by storm. After 651 performances in London the play went on a long tour; it was revived, again at the Coliseum, in 1940 and again toured, since when it has been seen as an ice-spectacle. In this present version, prepared for performance by Amateur Operatic Societies, the adaptors have added additional opportunities for both singing chorus, and dancers. With its many characters, colourful Tyrolean setting and costumes and glorious music, there can be no doubt that *White Horse Inn* remains one of the happiest and most exciting musical comedies of all time.

B. G.
E. M.

WHITE HORSE INN

MUSIC

ACT I

SCENE 1

Outside the " White Horse Inn ". Early morning on a Summer's day prior to 1914

The setting is a theatrical presentation of the internationally famous " White Horse Inn " (Im weissen Rössl) which stands on the shores of Lake Wolfgang in the Saltzhammergut province of Northern Austria. The Inn itself, a gaily painted building in the highly decorated style of the country, is L, with the main entrance facing R, under a practical balcony. From the balcony, french windows open into the principal guest-room. There is a small practical, dormer window over the french windows. Part of another building, the Mayor's house, stands R. It is in the same style with a deep, sloping roof, and with a balcony under which is a door leading into the building. French windows open on to the balcony. The backcloth shows an imposing view of the mountains across the Lake with villages and individual houses which will light up in the night scene. There are entrances not only from within the buildings, but above and below them, between fir-tree wings. Back C there is a rostrum from R to L approached by steps from the stage forming a landing-stage for the small steamers that call at the Inn. Between the landing-stage and the backcloth there are rails and sufficient space for the steamer to appear. Gaily painted tubs containing small trees decorate the entrance to the Inn and there are one or two small tables with chairs down L, outside the Inn.

INTRODUCTION

No. 1

KATHI, QUARTET and CHORUS

Immediately following the Overture the CURTAIN *rises to atmospheric music and yodelling off. The light for the moment is pale and shimmering. A distant bell is heard above the singing of the birds. A cock crows as the light increases.*

LIGHTING CUE 1

KATHI [*off · yodelling*] Holdrio, Holdrio, Holdrio.
CHORUS [*off; singing*] Ah, Ah, Ah, Ah, Ah.

A MAIDSERVANT *enters on the balcony* L *and shakes a rug : she is joined almost immediately by a second* MAID *who flicks a duster. They stand side by side enjoying the peace of the morning.*

MAIDS [*singing*] On meadow and lake
 At the dawn of the day,
 The shadows awake
 And creep swiftly away.

Sunlight now fills the stage. A MAN *enters down* R *with a wheelbarrow filled with potted flowers : he is followed by a second* MAN *carrying baskets filled to overflowing with fruit, vegetables, lobsters and other colourful provisions.*

 O'er valley and hill
 Not an echo is stirred,
 All's peaceful and still,
 Not a sound to be heard.

1ST MAN [*speaking over the music*] Good morning, Lilli.
1ST MAID [*speaking over the music*] Good morning, Hansi—what a beautiful day.

MEN [*singing*] On meadow and lake
 At the dawn of the day,
 The shadows awake
 And creep swiftly away.

QUARTET. O'er valley and hill
Not an echo is stirred,
All's peaceful and still,
Not a sound to be heard.

KATHI, yodelling, enters up R. She is the postwoman, a stalwart lady with a leather pouch slung over her shoulder.

KATHI } *[together]* {Holdrio, Holdrio, Holdrio, Holdrio.
QUARTET   {Ah, Ah, Ah.

The music continues. KATHI finishes on a loud and somewhat inaccurate note.

KARL, "piccolo" waiter and general busybody of the "White Horse Inn", enters hastily from the Inn. He is a small cheerful youth of about fourteen dressed in a dinner jacket and long white apron. He carries two gay check tablecloths.

KARL *[speaking over the music]* Hey, Kathi; not so much noise. You'll wake the whole hotel.

The two MAIDS, laughing, exit into the bedroom.

The two MEN, laughing, cross and exit up L.

KATHI. Why, aren't your people up yet?
KARL. No. They all turned over and went to sleep again. *[He moves to the tables down L and spreads the cloths on them]*

KATHI looks into her pouch.

CHORUS *[off; singing]*
On meadow and lake
At the dawn of the day,
The shadows awake
And creep swiftly away.
O'er valley and hill
Not an echo is stirred,
All's peaceful and still,
Not a sound to be heard.

KATHI *[taking a bundle of letters from her pouch]* Here's the mail for the *White Horse Inn.*

KARL moves to Kathi, takes the letters and searches hurriedly through them.

KARL. Bah! Not a word. The faithless hussy! You women. You're all alike.
KATHI. Perhaps she's found someone a bit younger.
KARL. Not her. As a matter of fact, she never learnt to write. Too busy minding the pigs!
KATHI. A pig-fancier, is she? And you're naturally a bit jealous.
KARL *[threatening her]* Now then! None of that if you want to live to enjoy your pension. *[He looks up L]* Hullo. Look who's here. *[He moves LC]*

KATHI moves RC.

A FORESTER enters up L and moves down C. He wears a green uniform, has a voluminous beard and carries a gun.

[He bows] Good morning, Mr Head Forester. *[He moves to L of the Forester and touches his beard]* I see you've brought part of the forest with you.
FORESTER *[bowing]* Good morning, young sir.
KARL. I trust your wife enjoys good health?
FORESTER. Thank you—yes.
KARL. And the dear children? And the dear rabbits? Plentiful, I hope?
FORESTER. There should be good sport tomorrow when the shooting season opens. If only the weather holds.
KARL. The weather? Just a moment. *[He crows loudly like a cock]*
FORESTER. What's all that about?

SCENE 1   WHITE HORSE INN

KARL. Wait for the echo. [*He turns and crows faintly*] There you are. Whenever you hear an echo, it means rain.   MUSIC

Bells are heard from a distant chapel off R.
ZENZI, *a goatherd, enters up* R. *She is aged fifteen, and is leading a goat.*

ZENZI [*as she enters; singing*]
    On meadow and lake
    At the dawn of the day,
    The shadows awake
    And creep softly away.

KATHI [*yodelling*] Holdrio. [*She moves down* R]
FORESTER [*crossing to Kathi*] Well, I must be moving on. Coming my way? [*He tries to put his arm round her*]
KATHI [*evading him*] If your way lies through the forest, no.
FORESTER. Then I'll go yours.

         KATHI *and the* FORESTER *exit down* R. ZENZI *moves down* C.

KARL [*moving to* L *of Zenzi*] At last! Faithless woman! Where were *you* all last night?
ZENZI. We were killing a pig, and somehow you were always in my thoughts.

REPRISE   No. 1a

ZENZI

KARL [*speaking over the music; to the Goat*] Did you hear that, Fritz? I bet your Nanny wouldn't insult you like that. [*To Zenzi*] I've done with women. All is over between us.
ZENZI [*shrugging; to the Goat*] Come along, Fritz. We're spurned, cast aside. [*She sings*]

    O'er valley and hill
    Not an echo is stirred,
    All's peaceful and still
    Not a sound to be heard.

         ZENZI *exits down* L.

ENTRANCE OF TOURISTS   No. 2

LEOPOLD and CHORUS

The rustic peace is now rudely disturbed by the sound of a charabanc driving up and grinding to a standstill off R, *with the honking of a klaxon horn and with the screeching of the* TOURISTS.

COURIER [*off* R; *shouting*] Wolfgangsee! All out!
KARL [*running to the Inn door and shouting*] Hi! Look alive there! Here's a bus-full of trippers.

The COURIER, *dressed in guide uniform, enters up* R. *He carries a small megaphone.*
FRANZ *enters from the Inn* L. *He is a very tall, thin waiter.*

FRANZ [*to Karl*] Coming, sir. Coming. [*He claps his hands peremptorily*]

Some WAITERS *enter down* L *carrying a long trestle table laid with plates, cups, rolls, butter, fruit, etc. They set the table at an angle* LC. *Other* WAITERS *enter down* L *carrying benches which they place above and below the table.*

The TOURISTS *enter up* R.

WHITE HORSE INN   ACT I

COURIER [*moving down* R; *through the megaphone*] Ladies and gentlemen—mesdames et messieurs—   MUSIC
meine Damen und Herren—ten minutes' stop for breakfast.

The TOURISTS, *with screams of hunger, dash at the table like a swarm of locusts fighting for places.*

KARL [*to Franz*] Hurry up! They're not here to enjoy themselves. They want breakfast. [*He calls into the Inn*] Herr Leopold. Where is Herr Leopold?

TOURISTS [*singing*] Hi, there! Waiter! Breakfast! Breakfast!

Some WAITRESSES *enter down* L, *carrying pots of coffee and jugs of milk.*

WAITRESSES.   One moment, please! All right! We're here!
No use to thump on the table.
We'll satisfy your appetite, no fear,
As far as we're able.

The WAITERS *and* WAITRESSES *serve food and coffee.*

COURIER [*speaking over the music*] Ladies and Gentlemen! This is the famous *White Horse Inn*, where thousands come every year for a rest cure.

TOURISTS [*yelling*] Coffee! Waiter! Waiter! Coffee!

COURIER [*spoken*] From here you get an uninterrupted view of the famous Wolfgang Lake, the pearl of Salzkammergut, five hundred feet deep, complete with swimming pools, fresh-water shrimps, sailing boats, rainbow trout, skating rink, stadium . . .

TOURISTS [*shouting*] Butter! Waiter! Waiter!

COURIER [*spoken*] On your right the famous Schnutzberg, on your left the Schnatzberg, in front of you the Schnitzberg, behind you the Poopsberg.

TOURISTS [*singing*]   Milk! Marmalade, please!
Jam! Marmalade, please.

COURIER [*spoken*] And now that you've seen everything worth seeing, we leave at once for Ischl, the famous summer residence of His Majesty the Emperor Francis Joseph.

The WAITRESSES *exit down* L.

TOURISTS [*singing*]   Hi! Waiter! Where's the waiter?
Bring the bill, please! Come on, Waiter!
Where's the bill, you wretched waiter?
Waiter! Waiter! Leopold! Where's Leopold?
Where's Leopold? Where's Leopold the waiter?

LEOPOLD *enters from the Inn.*

LEOPOLD [*singing*]   Really, I assure you,
There's no need to hurry.
I deplore your most impatient attitude.

TOURISTS.   Bring the bill, please, will you?

LEOPOLD.   I can settle your affairs
Without much worry.
If you excite yourselves
You won't digest your food.
The sun is shining bright,
And in the warm sunlight
On love alone one might be well content to feed.

SCENE 1   WHITE HORSE INN

And though you're anxious to depart,
Let me say, before you start,
If you had love within your heart,
No more you'd need.

MUSIC

As LEOPOLD *sings he makes out the bills and is paid by the* TOURISTS *seated below the table.*

Two buttered toasts, a pot of tea.
A slice of love—that's one and three.
A lemon sole, with sauce and frillings
A saucy look, that's just three schillings.
Some coffee, miss? With bread and cheese?
A tiny kiss—six pfennigs, please.
A slice of ham, and cherry jam?

The TOURISTS *seated above the table get impatient and sing*

TOURISTS.   Leopold!

LEOPOLD.   Coming, sir! Coming, miss. Here I am.

TOURISTS.   Leopold!

LEOPOLD.   Coming, sir! Thank you, miss. If you please.
            Coming, miss! Just a moment, madam.

TOURISTS.   Leopold! Leopold!

LEOPOLD.   There's no need for you to fret.
            A little patience.
            If you don't want to drive me absolutely mad.

ALL TOURISTS.   Waiter! Bring the bill—the bill, please.

LEOPOLD.   Silence, please, or you'll upset
            All my calculations.
            With such a row
            I can't see how a chap can add.

ALL TOURISTS.   Waiter! Bring the bill. Bring the bill.

LEOPOLD.   The sun it shines up there
            And love is in the air,
            So really I don't care
            How angry you may be.

The TOURISTS *above the table, rise.*

ALL TOURISTS.   Please hurry, for although
            We're rapid eaters,
            We've still to go
            Four hundred kilometres.

LEOPOLD.   I really cannot let you go
            Until I know how much you owe.

[*Spoken*] Sit down!

The TOURISTS *resume their seats.*

So, for half an hour or so, don't bother me.

LEOPOLD *moves* C *and sings the remainder of the lyric with emotion, and while he is singing, the* TOURISTS *rise and creep quietly out, one by one, up* R. *The* COURIER *follows them off.* KARL *pleads with them in mime as they go.*

    The sun, so round and gold,
    Looks like some coin, we're told,
    A tip that once of old,
    We waiters used to share.
    Today we have to seem content
    With just a measly ten per cent.
    I hope you've all been satisfied.
[*He turns, is surprised to find the Tourists have gone without tipping him, and shrugs his shoulders*]
    I don't care!

Pinchers! [*To the Waiters*] Clear that stuff away. Not a tip between the lot of them. How am I going to pay my income tax? [*To Karl*] And, by the bye, how much do I owe you, Chief?

FRANZ *and the* WAITERS *exit down* L, *taking the table and benches with them.*

KARL. Thirty-four fifty.
LEOPOLD [*looking amorously towards the Inn*] And all for her.
KARL. Take my advice, Herr Leopold, as man to man. Sending roses anonymously every day to Frau Josepha—it's madness. Women will be the ruin of us chaps.
LEOPOLD [*dreamily*] One woman, yes! She only has to speak to me in her soft, silvery voice—she only has to look at me with her flashing eyes—and I feel like a piece of wet fish.

JOSEPHA VOGELHUBER, *the landlady, enters from the Inn. She is young and buxom and wears a few roses in the bodice of her dress. With her back to the audience, she stands in the doorway and shouts angrily at someone within.*

JOSEPHA [*angrily*] Answer me back, will you? Take that!

The sound of a blow is heard.

And I'll crack you over the head, again, if I have any more of it.
LEOPOLD. Ah! That soft, silvery voice.

JOSEPHA *turns and crosses to* L *of Leopold.*

JOSEPHA. Ah, Leopold.
LEOPOLD [*swooning*] Those flashing eyes.
JOSEPHA. What did you serve as a sweet for dinner last evening?
LEOPOLD. A piece of wet fish.
JOSEPHA. What!
KARL [*moving* LC] You must forgive him, Frau Josepha. When we men are smitten with love, we say and do the silliest things.

KARL, *with mock dramatic action, exits to the Inn.*

JOSEPHA. What have we got for luncheon today?
LEOPOLD [*still dreaming*] Cocotte!
JOSEPHA. What!
LEOPOLD. Eggs cocotte. [*Dreamily*] Little eggs in little cocottes—I mean, in little pots; in tiny little pots. In tiny weeny . . .
JOSEPHA [*interrupting impatiently*] And what's the savoury?
LEOPOLD [*looking lovingly at her*] Angels——
JOSEPHA. Angels?
LEOPOLD. —on horseback. Lovely little angels on tiny little barebacks—on tiny weeny . . .

SCENE 1   WHITE HORSE INN

JOSEPHA. "Barebacks"? Leopold! What's the matter with you? Why do you look at me like that?

LEOPOLD *continues to gaze at Josepha*.

I don't mind that idiotic expression in the eyes of a calf; but I won't have it from my head waiter. Understand? [*She moves towards the Inn*]

LEOPOLD [*following Josepha; amorously*] Josepha—Josepha—*meine Malchen*—*meine Pupperl* . . .

JOSEPHA [*turning*] Hey! Hey! I am not your *Pupperl* or anything like it. To you I am Frau Maria Gabriela Josepha Vogelhuber—proprietress of the *White Horse Inn*. And while we're on the subject let me tell you something else. During the last three years, since my husband died, I have had no less than five head waiters. They all behaved perfectly well to start with, but when they began looking at me like a calf—I mean, like you—do you know what I did? [*Spiritedly*] I *sacked* them. [*She playfully takes his ear*] Be careful, Leopold, or perhaps you'll make up the half dozen.

LEOPOLD. I'd make up a baker's dozen for *you*. [*Amorously*] Frau Josepha—I'm simply bursting with . . .

JOSEPHA. You can't burst here.
LEOPOLD. But some day I shall have to . . .
JOSEPHA. Hold your tongue. I won't listen.
LEOPOLD. You must!
JOSEPHA. Must?
LEOPOLD. I'll *make* you. [*He seizes her by the wrists and holds her fast during the first verse of the song*]

"IT WOULD BE WONDERFUL"

JOSEPHA, LEOPOLD *and* GIRLS

LEOPOLD.
    Once again,
    And not perhaps in vain,
    You must be told the old, old story.
    Listen, pray,
    You cannot get away
    Until you've heard each word I say.
    It would be wonderful, indeed,
    If you could love as *I* love;
    If in your eyes I could but read
    Your heart's reply to *my* love.
    Then take the love that I am giving,
    And make my life worth living,
    For all my dreams would come true
    If I knew that you loved me, too.

JOSEPHA [*breaking loose from him*]
    Let me go!
    You must not treat me so!
    Recall the fate of late head waiters.
    I'm a mate
    You'll never captivate,
    For nothing comes to those who "wait".

LEOPOLD.
    It would be wonderful, indeed,
    If you could love, as I love;

JOSEPHA.
    Leopold, you're simply raving.

LEOPOLD.
    If in your eyes I could but read
    Your heart's reply to my love.

The two MAIDS *enter on the balcony* L *and listen*.

		MUSIC
JOSEPHA.	Leopold, how madly you're behaving.	
LEOPOLD.	Then take the love that I am giving,	
JOSEPHA.	You silly man!	
LEOPOLD.	And make my life worth living.	
JOSEPHA.	I never can! I've had enough of that love-making stuff. Leopold, I'm off.	

JOSEPHA exits to the Inn.
The WAITRESSES *and some other* MAIDS *enter down* L.

GIRLS [*spoken*] Poor Leopold. Handsome Leopold. [*They sing*]
It would be wonderful, indeed,
If you could love as we love;
If in your eyes we could but read
Your heart's reply to our love.
Then take the love that we are giving,
And make our lives worth living.

LEOPOLD. For all my dreams would come true
If I knew that you loved me, too.

GIRLS. For all our dreams would come true
If you loved me, too, if you loved me, too,
If you loved me, too.

LEOPOLD. All my dreams would come true
If you loved me, too.

LEOPOLD exits down R.
JOSEPHA enters from the Inn.

JOSEPHA [*to the Girls*] Now then, everything in order? Unless you girls look sweet enough to eat we shall lose our reputation. [*She calls commandingly*] Leopold.

LEOPOLD enters down R.

LEOPOLD. Coming, " sir ".
JOSEPHA. The boat will be in any moment, now—[*she points to the balcony* L] see that the Balcony room is got ready—number four. Fresh curtains, and roses on the dressing-table.

The two MAIDS *exit on the balcony. The* WAITRESSES *exit to the Inn. The other* MAIDS *group up* R.

LEOPOLD [*jealously*] Ah! Perhaps for the English gentleman—Herr Sutton—the solicitor from London? The late head waiter told me that you had a complex for him.
JOSEPHA. A complex? [*Lovingly*] He's our best client. Everybody loves him. He's already announced his intention of coming. [*She takes the roses from her bodice and tenderly caresses them*] Anonymously!
LEOPOLD. He has, has he? [*With increasing warmth*] Well, let me tell you this, Frau Maria Gabriela Josepha Vogelhuber—proprietress of the *White Horse Inn*—I had meant to carry the secret with me to the grave, but if you're going to wear my roses thinking that they come from this cussed solicitor of yours—then—I don't give a hoot.

The sound of the boat's siren is heard off L *in the distance.*

JOSEPHA. The boat!

SCENE 1   WHITE HORSE INN

LEOPOLD. Well, I'm glad *somebody's* giving a hoot.   MUSIC

The siren is heard nearer.

MAIDS [*excitedly*] The boat! The boat!
JOSEPHA [*indignantly*] What! Leopold! *You!* You dare to send me roses every day and to sign yourself " your loving Schnucky-doodle-ums " !

LEOPOLD *nods tenderly.*

Thank you very much. [*She throws the roses at Leopold's feet*] I don't give a hoot for your schnucky-doodle-ums. There!

The siren is heard nearer.

LEOPOLD [*picking up the roses; bitterly*] Frau Josepha—I'm bursting with . . .

The siren is heard very close and loud.

[*He crosses below Josepha to the Inn door*] Every time I start bursting there's that damned steamer.

LEOPOLD *exits to the Inn.*

JOSEPHA [*calling*] Waiter! Waiter!

FRANZ *and* KARL *enter from the Inn.*

FRANZ. Coming, madam.
JOSEPHA. There were six portions of curried carp over from last night. They must be got rid of. Luckily, these tourists will swallow anything.

JOSEPHA *exits to the Inn.*

KARL. Attention! Six portions of curried carp must be sold before they die on us.

KARL, *with a gesture of despair, exits to the Inn.* The *two* MAIDS *enter on the balcony* L. *The* WAITRESSES *enter down* L. *The* MAIDS *up* R *move down* R.

ARRIVAL OF THE GUESTS   No. 4

CHORUS

GIRLS [*singing*]   We maids can all be trusted
To keep the rooms well dusted.
We change and air the bedding;
We keep the moth from spreading.
Heigh ho!
Life is hard, you know,
For a Chambermaid is always on the go.

The ALPINE GUIDES *enter up* R. *They have alpenstocks and haversacks.*

GUIDES.   We scale the steepest rocks
With ropes and alpenstocks.
All those who climb
To heights sublime
Will, ev'ry time, engage us.
Where'er we go
They always know,
They're safe; we're so courageous.

The FLOWER SELLERS, *with baskets of flowers, enter down* R.
The HOTEL PORTERS *enter down* L.

		MUSIC
FLOWER GIRLS.	Many hours today we've spent Gath'ring flow'rs to bind in posies; Blooms whose scent may bring content To the most fastidious noses.	
PORTERS.	*Golden Dragon! Grand Hotel!* *Lake Pavilion! Mountain View!* *White Horse Inn*, as all know well, Is the best and cheapest, too.	
GUIDES.	We climb the steepest slopes With alpenstocks and ropes, And also telescopes, And also telescopes, telescopes.	
MAIDS.	We maids can all be trusted To keep the rooms well dusted. We change and air the bedding; We keep the moth from spreading.	
FLOWER GIRLS.	Tra-la-la, tra-la-la, We have flowers that are far Fairer than all others are.	
PORTERS.	*Golden Dragon! Grand Hotel!* At the *White Horse*, wise men dwell.	

The WAITERS *enter from the Inn and join in the singing.*

ALL.	This is the season of the year When bees go seeking honey, And like those bees, we're gathering here To make a pot of money. Now when tourists take their summer trips, We can batten and get fat on Tips, tips, tips. We raise our fees And that's why you hear Folks call this season And with good reason The " dearest " season of the year.

The Steamer appears above the rostrum from L *and stops* C. *On it are the* CAPTAIN, *two hefty* SAILORS, *some* TRAVELLERS *and a* HONEYMOON COUPLE. *The* SAILORS *make the boat fast with ropes: the* TRAVELLERS *disembark and come down* C. *They carry small luggage. The* PORTERS, GUIDES *and* FLOWER SELLERS *crowd around the Travellers, shouting and yelling.*

PORTERS.	*Golden Dragon! White Horse Inn*, sirs! *White Horse Inn*, sirs! *White Horse Inn*, sirs! *White Horse Inn!* Up the highest mountains Trips taken daily. *White Horse, White Horse Inn.*

SCENE 1	WHITE HORSE INN	

GUIDES.	*The Palace Hotel!* The finest hotel! *The Old Silver Bell!* The finest hotel! *Golden Dragon! White Horse Inn! Golden Dragon! White Horse Inn!* Trips are daily taken Up the highest mountains To the very top.	MUSIC
MAIDS.	We maids can all be trusted To keep the rooms well dusted. We change and air the bedding; We keep the moth from spreading. *White Horse Inn,* sir! *Silver Bell,* sir! *Golden Dragon! White Horse, White Horse Inn.*	
FLOWER GIRLS.	Tra-la-la, tra-la-la. We have flowers. Tra-la-la, tra-la-la. We have flowers. Tra-la-la, tra-la-la. We have flowers. Tra-la-la, tra-la-la. See how fair our flowers are. Tra-la-la, tra-la-la. See how fair, How fair our flowers are.	
ALL.	This is the season of the year When bees go seeking honey, And like those bees, we're gathering here To make a pot of money. Now when tourists take their summer trips, We can batten and get fat on Tips, tips, tips. We raise our fees And that's why you hear Folks call this season And with good reason The " dearest " season of the year.	

The TRAVELLERS, FLOWER SELLERS, GUIDES, MAIDS, WAITRESSES, PORTERS, WAITERS *and* FRANZ *drift off by all exits. The* CAPTAIN *and the two* SAILORS *exit up* L. *The* HONEYMOON COUPLE *disembark and come down* C, *arm-in-arm, gazing at each other.*

LEOPOLD *and* KARL *enter from the Inn.*

LEOPOLD [*to the Bridegroom*] Welcome to the *White Horse Inn.* Would you prefer a room in the main building or in the annexe?
BRIDEGROOM [*gazing into the Bride's eyes*] It's all the same to us.
LEOPOLD [*to the Bride*] Or one with a view over the lake?
BRIDE [*gazing into the Bridegroom's eyes*] It's all the same to us.
LEOPOLD. Would you care for a little refreshment?
BRIDEGROOM. It's all the same to us.
LEOPOLD [*to Karl*] Two portions of curried carp, quick.

KARL [*calling into the Inn*] Curried carp twice for room thirty-six.

MUSIC

KARL exits to the Inn. The HONEYMOON COUPLE *cross towards the Inn door.*

LEOPOLD. Wait a minute! Number thirty-six has only a single bed.
BRIDEGROOM }
BRIDE   [*together*] It's all the same to us.

JOSEPHA enters on the balcony L. *The* HONEYMOON COUPLE *exit to the Inn.*

LEOPOLD [*looking up at Josepha*] Your Herr Sutton wasn't on the boat after all?
JOSEPHA. Don't worry. He'll come by the afternoon boat. The Balcony room must be kept for him, understand?
LEOPOLD. But supposing . . .
JOSEPHA. Silence! Who gives orders here? You or I?
LEOPOLD. It's all the same to us.

LEOPOLD exits to the Inn. JOSEPHA shrugs with annoyance and exits from the balcony. Considerable noise is heard off up L.

JOHN EBENEZER GRINKLE and his daughter OTTOLINE enter up L. *GRINKLE is a choleric, paunchy, North Country business man. He wears a light summer suit and a straw hat with a very " loud " ribbon, into which are stuck two steamer tickets. He carries two bags. He is being restrained by the two SAILORS and admonished by the CAPTAIN. OTTOLINE is a pretty young girl, very attractive in spite of clothes that are " not quite ". She carries a light case.*

GRINKLE [*as he enters; struggling*] Let go of me! Take your hands off. [*He moves down* C] Send for the British Consul. [*He puts down his bags*]
OTTOLINE [L *of Grinkle; distressed*] Father, please! [*To the Captain*] What's the matter? What do you want? [*She puts down her case*]
CAPTAIN [*down* R *of Grinkle; stolidly*] Fahrkarte.
GRINKLE [*indignantly*] What's that?
SAILORS [*together*] Fahrkarte.
GRINKLE. Far-carter? I never heard such language in my life.
OTTOLINE. But, Father, you don't know what it means. [*She takes a pocket dictionary from her handbag*]
GRINKLE. No, but I've a pretty good idea. They want us to buzz off!
OTTOLINE. How do you spell it? [*She riffles through the dictionary*]
GRINKLE [*in a voice of thunder*] Don't tell her.
OTTOLINE. Ah, here it is. " Fahrkarte." Daddy, do you know what it means?
GRINKLE [*covering his ears*] Ottoline, I forbid you to soil your lips.
OTTOLINE [*laughing*] Don't be silly. They only want the *tickets*.
GRINKLE. Th-th-the—t-t-tickets?
CAPTAIN }
SAILORS   [*together; nodding*] Ja! Ja!
GRINKLE. Then why didn't they say so? Tickets? Tickets? [*He searches in his pockets*]

There is comedy business as OTTOLINE joins in the search, spins him round, puts her hand in his hip pocket and tickles him.

[*He giggles*] Ee! Give-over!

The CAPTAIN and the SAILORS wait stolidly and rather menacingly.

OTTOLINE [*seeing the tickets in Grinkle's hat-band*] Daddy—your hat.
GRINKLE. Well, what's the matter with it?
OTTOLINE. The tickets.

GRINKLE removes his hat, sees the tickets and takes them out.

GRINKLE. There now! Why didn't you tell me? [*He thrusts the tickets at the Captain*] There you are. Take 'em.

SCENE 1 — WHITE HORSE INN

CAPTAIN [*taking the tickets*] Danke, mein Herr. [*He bows*]'
The CAPTAIN *and the* SAILORS *exit up* L.
GRINKLE [*shouting after the Captain*] Far-carter! And the same to you. [*He grumbles*] Six bob for a trip on that bumboat. We could have travelled from Oldham to Eccles and back for half the money. [*He mops his brow*] Oh, why didn't we go to Clacton? [*Or local reference*]
LEOPOLD *enters from the Inn. He has a napkin over his arm.*
OTTOLINE [*moving up* c] But, Daddy, look at the lovely lake.
GRINKLE [*turning and looking up* c] Call that a lake? Bah! It's nothing but a puddle. [*He puts his hat on his head*]
LEOPOLD *moves down* L *of Grinkle.*
OTTOLINE. And just sniff that glorious mountain air. [*She breathes deeply*]
GRINKLE [*sniffing*] Air? Why, it smells like . . . [*He turns, finds himself face to face with Leopold and starts back suspiciously*]
LEOPOLD. You are from England, I see.
GRINKLE [*to Ottoline*] How did he know that?
OTTOLINE *moves to* R *of Grinkle.*
LEOPOLD [*indicating Grinkle's hat-band*] The honourable cycling club.
GRINKLE [*furiously*] Cycling club? [*He removes his hat*] Young man, allow me to tell you that those are the colours of . . . [*Local allusion*] Cycling club! That's the second insult I've received since I stepped ashore.
OTTOLINE [*sweetly*] They say everything goes in threes.
GRINKLE *glares at Ottoline.*
GRINKLE [*to Leopold*] Well. What have you got to eat?
LEOPOLD. We've some excellent curried carp—quite fresh yesterday.
GRINKLE. Curried carp? With my delicate digestion? Have you any pig's trotters or tripe? I don't suppose they've ever heard of tripe. Oh, why did we ever leave Oldham?
OTTOLINE. But, Papa, look at the lovely snow—the eternal snow.
GRINKLE. Who wants to look at snow? Eternal, too. In England we're only too glad when there isn't any, and here you've got to be glad when there is. [*To Leopold*] What about rooms? I want two rooms—one with a balcony. I'm easily upset, as perhaps you've noticed. And when I'm upset I need a balcony.
LEOPOLD [*looking up at the balcony* L] We've only one room with a balcony.
GRINKLE. That will do.
LEOPOLD. But it's already engaged.
GRINKLE [*angrily*] Only one room with a balcony and you call this a hotel. In Clacton *every* room has a balcony—some of them have *three*. [*He moves angrily up* c]
OTTOLINE. Don't get excited, Papa.
LEOPOLD *moves to* L *of Ottoline, takes two forms and a fountain pen from his pocket and hands them to her.*
Shall I fill up these forms? [*She crosses and sits at the table down* L]
GRINKLE [*moving down* c] Forms! Why on earth? Nobody in Oldham has to fill up forms. But here, what with these infernal forms, and eternal snow . . .
OTTOLINE. Oh, Papa! [*She writes*] "John Ebenezer Grinkle and daughter." [*She reads*] "Profession." Shall I put "Manufacturer"?
GRINKLE. Naturally. You might add "Underwear" in brackets.
OTTOLINE [*writing*] "Underwear", in brackets—"Oldham".
LEOPOLD. So you are Mr Grinkle? Excuse me. There's a telegram for you, sir. I'll fetch it.
LEOPOLD *exits quickly to the Inn.*

GRINKLE. A telegram. Probably from that old scoundrel Smith of Hammersmith. How I hate that man! There's only one man I hate more and that's his solicitor, that chap Sutton.

OTTOLINE. I never understand why.
GRINKLE. Good Lord—haven't I told you a hundred times? You know my patent underwear—the "Apollo" combination, one-piece "Vestiknicks" that buttons up the front? Well, hardly had I put this wonderful invention on the market before that old scoundrel Smith comes along with a rival underwear—the "Hercules" combination, one piece "Shirtopants", buttoning up the *back*. Then the fight began—a struggle to the death—front or back, which would win?

> LEOPOLD *enters from the Inn and moves to* L *of Grinkle. He carries a telegram.*

And that scoundrel of a Sutton has the nerve to back the back.
LEOPOLD. Excuse me, sir, but did I hear you use the expression "scoundrel" in connexion with the solicitor—Mr Sutton?
GRINKLE [*taking the telegram from Leopold*] What's it got to do with thee? Mind your own business. [*He opens the telegram and reads*] "Sutton advises me resist your ridiculous claim. Communicate with him direct. Smith, Shirtopants, Hammersmith."

> LEOPOLD *crosses above Grinkle to* R *of him.* KARL *enters from the Inn, and moves to* L *of Grinkle. He carries a dish with a silver cover.*

[*Furiously*] Sutton! Sutton! I'd like to . . .

> KARL *puts the dish under Grinkle's nose and lifts the cover.*

[*He gasps*] Good God, what's that?
KARL. Curried carp.
GRINKLE. Well, you "curry" it back to the kitchen.
LEOPOLD [*to Karl*] Get out! We can't give a gentleman like this yesterday's carp.
KARL [*moving to the Inn door; smelling the carp*] It'll be too late tomorrow.

> KARL *bangs the cover over the dish and exits to the Inn.*

LEOPOLD. I'll bring you something really tasty to your room. [*He pauses, suddenly inspired, and snaps his fingers*] And what a room! Number four, the Balcony room.
GRINKLE. But I thought you said it was engaged.
LEOPOLD. So it is. For *you*. Directly you hove in sight I said to myself, "I'll reserve a room with a balcony for that good, kind, distinguished-looking gentleman."
GRINKLE. Good?
LEOPOLD. Certainly.
GRINKLE. Kind?
LEOPOLD. Yes, and distinguished-looking.
GRINKLE. Ee! That's the far-carter. Well, and what food are you going to bring up to us?
LEOPOLD [*very rapidly*] I suggest "Backhandl-mit-gurkensalat".
GRINKLE. Don't be filthy! None of your backhandles for me. Have you got any smoked flounders? But I suppose you foreigners don't smoke flounders here.
LEOPOLD. The guests usually prefer cigars.
GRINKLE. What about Lancashire hot-pot?
LEOPOLD. "Lankyhottentot"? Never heard of it.

> OTTOLINE *rises and moves* LC.

GRINKLE. Never heard of Lancashire hot-pot? You've never lived. Why in heaven's name didn't we go to Clacton?

> GRINKLE *and* OTTOLINE *pick up their luggage and exit to the Inn.*
>
> KARL *enters down* L *and crosses to Leopold.*

KARL. Leopold. Herr Sutton is arriving. Where is he to sleep? [*He goes up* L *and looks off*]
LEOPOLD. Herr Sutton! We're full up. He'll have to sleep in the cow-shed.
KARL. Perhaps the cows will object. [*He turns*] Here he comes now. [*He moves quickly to Leopold and pushes him to the Inn door*]

SCENE 1   WHITE HORSE INN   15

LEOPOLD [*as they go*]   Herr Sutton! I'll make Yankeedoodle hot-pot of Herr Sutton.   MUSIC

      KARL *and* LEOPOLD *exit to the Inn.*
      VALENTINE SUTTON *enters up* L. *He is aged twenty-five and wears a grey flannel suit. He carries a smart suitcase which he puts down up* LC. *He comes in gaily, pleased with himself and all the world and at once sings.*

    "THE WHITE HORSE INN"   No. 5

    SUTTON, JOSEPHA, CHORUS *and* DANCERS

SUTTON. When there comes the time for summer holidays,
    And ev'ry wise man prays
    For change of air,
    There's a spot for which I'm not ashamed to sigh
    For well content am I
    When I fly there.
        JOSEPHA *enters from the Inn.*
    The *White Horse Inn!* At the *White Horse Inn,*
    There's joy the whole summer through.
    There's sunshine ever in store there,
    For happiness stands at the door there.
    The days fly past,
    You must leave at last,
    But still, whatever you do,
    You'll hear, when twilight is falling,
    The *White Horse* calling to you.
        JOSEPHA *smiles and moves to* L *of Sutton.*
        A PORTER *enters from the Inn, picks up Sutton's suitcase and exits with it to the Inn.*

JOSEPHA. You will find a welcome kind awaiting you,
    From hearts as fond and true
    As ever beat.
    Happy still though up the hill your path may wend,
    For at the journey's end
    Faithful friends meet.
        The CHORUS *enter in speciality costumes.*
BOTH.   The *White Horse Inn!* At the *White Horse Inn,*
    There's joy the whole summer through.
    There's sunshine ever in store there,
    For happiness stands at the door there.

ALL.   The days fly past,
    You must leave at last,
    But still, whatever you do,
    You'll hear, when twilight is falling,
    The *White Horse* calling to you.
        The DANCERS *enter, and dance. This continues until the end of the number.*
    The *White Horse Inn,* at the *White Horse Inn,*
    There's joy the whole summer through.
    There's sunshine ever in store there,
    For happiness stands at the door there.

The days fly past,
You must leave at last,
But still, whatever you do,
You'll hear, when twilight is falling,
The *White Horse* calling to you.
The *White Horse Inn*.

MUSIC

The number and Dance ends in a picture.

EXIT MUSIC

No. 5a

ALL [*singing as they go*]
You'll hear when twilight is falling,
The *White Horse* calling to you.

JOSEPHA, *the* CHORUS *and the* DANCERS *exit*. SUTTON *moves* C.
LEOPOLD *enters from the Inn and crosses to* L *of Sutton.*

SUTTON [*gaily*] Are you the new head waiter?
LEOPOLD. Leopold is the name. Herr Sutton, I believe?
SUTTON. Correct. I hope you'll give satisfaction.
LEOPOLD [*aside*] I hope I'll get it.
SUTTON. How's the weather this year?
LEOPOLD. Terrible. Rain. Nothing but rain.
SUTTON. Good. I'm used to it. I come from London.
LEOPOLD. And snow, too. Lots of snow.
SUTTON. Excellent! I love snow. And the cooking?
LEOPOLD. Filthy! Our new chef's a dying man.
SUTTON. Dear me! What's he dying of?
LEOPOLD. Starvation. He just can't eat anything he cooks himself, and he's no time to eat out.
SUTTON. Otherwise I suppose the *White Horse* is still as comfortable?
LEOPOLD. The mosquitoes are terrible this year. The beds are too short, the moth have played havoc with the blankets and we're expecting an earthquake any moment.
SUTTON. It'll be a new experience.

GRINKLE *enters on the balcony* L.

And now—back to my old Balcony room. [*He throws his hat on to the balcony* L]

GRINKLE *catches Sutton's hat.*

GRINKLE. Excuse me, young man, but I think this is your hat. [*He throws the hat down to Sutton*] The cloakroom is downstairs.
SUTTON [*to Leopold*] What's that on my balcony?
GRINKLE [*overhearing*] What do you say? *Your* balcony! This is *my* balcony.
SUTTON. You'll pardon me, but that's *my* room you're in.

JOSEPHA *enters from the Inn.*

GRINKLE. Can't you *see* it's already occupied?
JOSEPHA [*to Grinkle*] Excuse me, sir, but may I enquire who showed you up there?
GRINKLE. Your head waiter, of course.

LEOPOLD *tries to steal off* R.

JOSEPHA. Leopold? [*She advances threateningly on Leopold*] Did *you* give this gentleman Number four?
LEOPOLD. Of course. I couldn't leave a gentleman with such a lovely bay-window—[*he indicates a large paunch*] without a balcony to put round it. I—I think I heard a bell. [*He turns to the Inn and calls*] Coming, sir. Coming.

LEOPOLD *exits hurriedly to the Inn.*

JOSEPHA [*to Grinkle*] I am very sorry, sir, but—[*she points to Sutton*] this gentleman has had that MUSIC room for the last six summers.
GRINKLE. Then seven must be his unlucky number.
SUTTON. And I may tell you—[*he takes a telegram from his pocket*] I have an official acknowledgment. As a lawyer, I strongly advise you . . .
GRINKLE [*breaking in*] A lawyer. Don't you try selling any advice to me.
JOSEPHA. I'm sorry. I promised that room to this gentleman, and a woman never breaks her promise.
GRINKLE [*disregarding this and airily singing to himself*] Toodle-oodle-oo, Toodle-oodle-ay.
JOSEPHA. You refuse to move?

GRINKLE continues to sing.

Very well, then. [*She calls*] Johann. Martin.
GRINKLE. Ha! You can send up all your weak-kneed, under-fed staff. I'm not moving.

Two enormously muscular SERVANTS *enter down* L.

JOSEPHA [*to the Servants*] Fetch down the luggage from Number Four, please. Should you meet with any resistance from the gentleman already in the room, just deal with him in the usual manner.

The two SERVANTS *roll up their sleeves.* GRINKLE *turns and sees the Servants.*

GRINKLE. Good Heavens! [*He leans over the balcony rail*] Oh. Steward!

The SERVANTS *exit to the Inn.* GRINKLE, *with his hand on his forehead, staggers into the room.*
OTTOLINE enters from the Inn. GRINKLE *re-appears backwards from the room.*

[*He speaks into the room*] Certainly. Not at all. It's a pleasure. [*He turns and sees Ottoline*] Ottoline, we're moving. [*He points to Sutton*] That kind gentleman there is turning us out.

The SERVANTS *enter from the Inn. They carry Grinkle's bags and Ottoline's case.*

OTTOLINE. Did you say "gentleman", Papa?
SUTTON [*bowing to Ottoline*] I'm sorry.

GRINKLE exits into the room.

I had no idea there was a lady in the balcony room—and such a charming lady, too. I'm only too delighted to give it up. [*To the Servants*] Take the luggage back again.

The SERVANTS *turn to go.*
GRINKLE enters from the Inn and bumps into the Servants.
The SERVANTS *exit with the luggage to the Inn.*

JOSEPHA. I beg your pardon, I can't allow this. The room is yours, Herr Sutton—you know that. [*She calls*] Johann. Martin.

The SERVANTS, *still holding the luggage, enter from the Inn.*

GRINKLE [*watching the Servants*] What are they up to? Is this a game or something?
OTTOLINE [*pointing to Sutton*] This gentleman has very charmingly consented to give up his room.
GRINKLE. Oh, indeed! He's charming enough to *you*—but he gives me a pain in the neck. [*To the Servants*] Put that luggage down again.

The SERVANTS *set down the luggage.*

OTTOLINE. Really, Papa, you must be sensible. I want to stay here. I won't go to Clacton. [*To the Servants*] Take those things upstairs, please.

The SERVANTS *pick up the luggage and exit to the Inn.*

JOSEPHA. I see I shall have to give up my room to Mr Sutton.
GRINKLE. Just a moment. I didn't quite catch—what did you say?

SUTTON. Allow me to introduce myself. Valentine Sutton—of the Lincoln's Inn firm of Sutton, Sutton, Sutton and Sutton.   MUSIC

The SERVANTS *enter on the balcony* L *with the luggage.*

GRINKLE [*shouting*] So! You're Sutton, of Sutton, Sutton, Sutton——
OTTOLINE. Control yourself, Papa.
GRINKLE. —and Sutton. [*To the Servants on the balcony*] Bring that stuff down at once.
SUTTON. But—I don't understand . . .
GRINKLE. Don't you? Well, you soon will. My name is Grinkle—John Ebenezer Grinkle—of Oldham.
SUTTON. What! You're the "Apollo patent combination Vestinicks"?
GRINKLE. Yes. And I button up the front, don't forget that. And do you think I'm going to stay in the same house as a man who buttons up the back? [*To the Servants*] My luggage.

The SERVANTS, *by this time thoroughly bored by the whole business, throw the luggage over the balcony rail.*

OTTOLINE ⎫   ⎧ My case!
GRINKLE ⎬ [*together*] ⎨ Hi! Stop that!
SUTTON   ⎭   ⎩ Just a moment! I'll arrange things.

LEOPOLD *and* KARL *enter from the Inn.* LEOPOLD *is hit by a case from the balcony.* GRINKLE *collects the luggage.*

The SERVANTS *exit from the balcony.*

JOSEPHA, GRINKLE, OTTOLINE *and* SUTTON, *arguing and quarrelling, exit to the Inn.* KARL *jumps into Leopold's arms.*

LEOPOLD. And it's all the fault of that wretched Sutton fellow. [*He drops Karl to the ground*] If only I could put her off him somehow.
KARL. But, Leopold, didn't you notice him making eyes at the young lady from England?
LEOPOLD. What? You mean the solicitor was drawn to the daughter of my old friend Grinkle?
KARL. As soon as their eyes met it was love at first sight.
LEOPOLD. Ah! What a lovely sight.

OTTOLINE *enters from the Inn.*

GRINKLE'S *head appears out of the small window at the top of the Inn building* L.

GRINKLE. Hey! Help! Look what they've done to me. They've put me in the pigeon loft.
OTTOLINE [*laughing*] Daddy, you look a perfect picture up there.
GRINKLE. A picture! You mean I've been framed. You said something just now about a *third* insult. Well, here it is. [*He holds out a spray of white roses*] White roses on my dressing-table. White roses—for a lad from Lancashire. [*He throws the roses down*] Pack my traps at once—we're leaving.
OTTOLINE [*picking up the roses*] Oh, no, we're not.
GRINKLE. Don't you dare contradict your favourite father. I'm off to Clacton.

GRINKLE *disappears from the window.* OTTOLINE, LEOPOLD *and* KARL *move down* C.

OTTOLINE. You may be, but—[*she smells the roses*] I'm stopping here—at Wolfgang on the lake.

The RUNNING TABS *close behind Leopold, Ottoline and Karl*

LEOPOLD [*to Ottoline*] Bravo! Bravo!

MELOS

No. 5b

[*Over the music*] And I think I know the very place for you.
OTTOLINE. A boarding-house?
LEOPOLD. Not exactly.
OTTOLINE. A smart hotel?

SCENE 2   WHITE HORSE INN   19

LEOPOLD. You'll love it. Only a stone's throw away. Follow that path to the right and I'll be   MUSIC
with you in a moment.
OTTOLINE [*crossing to* R] I'm very curious.
          OTTOLINE *exits* R.
KARL. Where are you sending her?
LEOPOLD. Just pop across to Herr Sutton and tell him the young English lady is waiting for him in the cow-shed.
KARL. In the cow-shed?
LEOPOLD. In the cow-shed. Can you imagine a more exciting place for a rendezvous?
KARL. Not if I were a bull.
          KARL *exits* L.
          LEOPOLD *exits* R.

SCENE 2

The cow-shed

The setting is a front cloth depicting the outside of the cow-shed. There are three profile cows, C, RC *and* LC. *They have movable heads, eyes and tails. Milkmaids' stools are set by each cow.*
When the RUNNING TABS *open, the mooing of the cows is heard. The* DAIRYMAIDS *are milking the cows and standing by, singing.*

"HAPPY COWS"   No. 6
DAIRYMAIDS *and* DANCERS

DAIRYMAIDS.   Down in the meadow when Spring comes along,
There is life to be lived to the full.
Sweet are the cow-bells, the world is a song,
There's romance in the glance of a bull.
Each pretty maid moos a soft serenade,
Swishing her tail with delight,
Pastured in Heaven where nothing goes wrong,
And love alone can be right.
Happy cows,
As you browse,
Nought can rouse you from your dreams,
And although,
As we know,
Life is slow, how safe it seems.
All you do
Is to moo
And to chew the new-mown hay;
It's so calm
On the farm
And no harm can come your way.
          The DANCERS, *as* FARMHANDS, *enter and a Clog Dance follows.*
          At the end of the Dance all exit L.
          LEOPOLD *and* OTTOLINE *enter* R.
LEOPOLD. There you are.
OTTOLINE. Is this your " smart hotel "?

LEOPOLD. I'll explain it all.

A cow moos.

[*He pushes away the head of a cow that is in his way*] Excuse me. You ought not to drive on your horn.
[*To Ottoline*] It's like this. Herr Sutton—the solicitor . . .
OTTOLINE. Don't talk to me about that man. Now he's spoiling Papa's holiday, too.
LEOPOLD. Would you like to alter the whole situation—just like that? [*He snaps his fingers*] You've only got to flirt with him.
OTTOLINE. Me flirt?
LEOPOLD. And take him off Josepha's—I mean off your father's hands.
OTTOLINE [*thinking it over*] Of course—he *is* rather nice-looking.
LEOPOLD. Don't change your mind. He'll be along any minute.
OTTOLINE [*startled*] You mean he's coming *here*.
LEOPOLD. Yes. And he should find a cow-shed quite a home-from-home—he's been milking his clients for years.

SUTTON *enters* R.

OTTOLINE. Just bring your Mr Sutton here—*I'll* teach him how to milk cows.
SUTTON. He's waiting to be taught.
LEOPOLD [*patting a cow*] Don't let them overwork you, Daisy. Unfortunately, old girl—[*he mimes the milking of a cow*] warm hearts mean cold hands.

LEOPOLD *exits* L.

OTTOLINE. So—you're the famous solicitor. Are you starting an action against *me*, Mr Valentine Sutton?

"YOUR EYES" No. 7

SUTTON, OTTOLINE, CHORUS *and* DANCERS

SUTTON [*speaking over the music*] Action, indeed! I certainly thought of bringing a suit—I shall open my case by calling the skies as witness to prove—that none has ever looked into fairer eyes than yours.

OTTOLINE *turns away, but* SUTTON *takes her by the shoulders, turns her round and leads her down* C.

The RUNNING TABS *close behind Ottoline and Sutton*

SUTTON [*singing*] I scarcely would dare
To gaze in your eyes,
For well I'm aware
That Heaven within them lies.
And yet, if I do,
The light that I see
Colours the world anew
For me.
Your eyes have brought a deeper blue
To skies that caught their tender hue:
Where they mark the ground
There's a larkspur found,
And a cornflow'r is born
Or a blue-bell.
In shady glade or dewy grot
They paint each faint forget-me-not.
And the Spring breaks through
As I gaze into
Your eyes, so wise, so blue.

SCENE 3 — WHITE HORSE INN

OTTOLINE.   Some men, so they say   MUSIC
            Are equally keen
            On eyes that are grey
            Or hazel, or even green.
            No girl of today
            Knows which men prefer
            Until she has heard one say
            To her:

BOTH.   Your eyes have brought a deeper blue
            To skies that caught their tender hue:
            Where they mark the ground
            There's a larkspur found,
            And a cornflow'r is born
            Or a blue-bell.
            In shady glade or dewy grot
            They paint each faint forget-me-not.

The RUNNING TABS *open*

SCENE 3

Outside the Inn

When the RUNNING TABS *open, the* DANCERS, *dressed in blue, are revealed posed ready for the Dance that follows. The whole stage is flooded with blue light.* OTTOLINE *and* SUTTON *move up* C *between the Dancers, singing the last two lines.*

BOTH.   And the Spring breaks through
            As I gaze into
            Your eyes, so wise, so blue.

The DANCERS *dance a " soft-shoe " dance. At the end of the Dance* OTTOLINE *and* SUTTON *move down* C.

The GUESTS, MAIDS, WAITERS, *etc., enter.*

ALL.   Your eyes have brought a deeper blue
            To skies that caught their tender hue:
            Where they mark the ground
            There's a larkspur found,
            And a cornflow'r is born
            Or a blue-bell.
            In shady glade or dewy grot
            They paint each faint forget-me-not.
            And the Spring breaks through
            As I gaze into
            Your eyes, so wise, so blue
            Your eyes so blue.
            Your eyes so blue.

By the end of the refrain, ALL *have made their exit.*
The lights change to sunlight.

LIGHTING CUE 2

LEOPOLD *enters* R, *singing cheerfully and rubbing his hands as he watches* OTTOLINE *and* SUTTON *exit hand in hand.*

LEOPOLD [*singing*]   The cows are blue and so are you.

FINALE ACT I

<small>MUSIC
No. 8</small>

LEOPOLD *and* CHORUS

JOSEPHA *enters from the Inn.*

JOSEPHA [*speaking over the music*] Leopold! Where have you been?
LEOPOLD [*amorously*] Josepha! [*He tries to kiss her*]
JOSEPHA [*disengaging herself*] You must be mad. The whole hotel full of people, and you don't seem to care. It's always the same.
          LEOPOLD *goes on to his knees.*
LEOPOLD [*pleadingly*] Josepha—won't you give me just *one?*
JOSEPHA [*moving slightly* L] Leopold!
LEOPOLD [*following her; still on his knees*] Half a one.
JOSEPHA. Are you mad?
LEOPOLD. Yes. A waiter is a human being, after all. Josepha! One little token of your affection—one little touch of your hand.
JOSEPHA. One touch of my hand? Is that all you want? Very well, then. [*She gives Leopold a resounding box on the ear*]
          LEOPOLD *collapses.*
Can't he ever let me alone?
         JOSEPHA *exits to the Inn.* LEOPOLD *rises, swathes his napkin round his face and sings with the* CHORUS *singing off.*

LEOPOLD. It would be wonderful, indeed,
     If you could love as I love;
     If in your eyes I could but read
     Your heart's reply to my love.

CHORUS [*off*] To take, instead of always giving
     Would make my life worth living,
LEOPOLD. For all my dreams could come true
     If I knew that you loved me, too.

          LEOPOLD *exits* R.
        The GUESTS *enter* L. *They carry umbrellas.*

GUESTS. This is the season of the year
     When bees go seeking honey,
     And like those bees, the good people here,
     Can make a lot of money.
     When we tourists take our Summer trips,
     They can batten and grow fat on
     Tips, tips, tips.

     They raise the fees
     And that's why you hear
     Folks call this season
     And with good reason
     The " dearest " season of the year.

GUESTS [*shouting*] Waiter! Waiter! Waiter!
       The WAITERS *and* WAITRESSES *enter. During the following verse, the lights fade to storm effect.*
             LIGHTING CUE 3

ALL. The *White Horse Inn!*
    Oh, the *White Horse Inn,*
    It's dull and dingy and small.

SCENE 8   WHITE HORSE INN

MUSIC

           The waiting's frightfully slack there,
           And no-one could ever go back there.
           Your bill you'd pay
           But you wait all day,
           For no-one comes to your call;
           The service is really appalling,
           It's no use calling at all.
           Leopold!
           Will you bring the bill?
           We're waiting until
           You bring us the bill.
           Leopold!

                    LEOPOLD *enters* R.

LEOPOLD [*quietly*]   Gentlemen and ladies, pray,
           Don't get excited.
           Please remember that a waiter is a man.
GUESTS.   Bring the bill, please, will you?
LEOPOLD.   On this lovely Summer's day.

             There is a flash of lightning and a peal of thunder.

LIGHTING CUE 4

           I'm quite delighted
           To be of any kind of service that I can.
           The sun is shining bright.

                  There is a clap of thunder.

           That gave me quite a fright.

             There is a flash of lightning and a peal of thunder.

LIGHTING CUE 5

           I think I'll say good night.

             LEOPOLD *moves to the Inn to exit, but is stopped by some of the*
             GUESTS. *During the final singing, the storm increases in violence.*

LIGHTING CUE 6

GUESTS.   This is the season of the year
           For lightning and for thunder.
           There are no trees to shelter us here,
           There's nothing to get under.
           There's a big storm brewing, that is plain.
           There's no doubt, that it's about
           To rain, rain, rain.

             It commences to rain. The GUESTS *open their umbrellas.*

           Though it's not much use complaining,
           We already feel the drops,
           And if once it starts a-raining
           It never, never stops.
           Oh, we wonder why we ever
           Dared to venture out of doors,
           In this climate where it never
           Never rains unless it pours.
           Oh, my! What shall we do?
           Oh, my! We'll get wet through.

Lucky fellers with umbrellas
May manage to keep dry,
But still the rain keeps falling,
Falling, falling from the sky.

Oh, it's not much use complaining,
We already feel the drops,
And if once it starts a-raining
It never, never stops.
Oh, we wonder why we ever
Dared to venture out of doors,
In this climate where it never
Never rains unless it pours.
Oh, my! What shall we do?
Oh, my! We'll get wet through.
Lucky fellers, with umbrellas
May manage to keep dry,
But still the rain keeps falling,
Falling, falling from the sky.

Oh, it's not much use complaining,
But what very heavy drops,
And if once it starts a-raining
It never, never stops.
Oh, we wonder why we ever
Dared to venture out of doors,
In this climate where it never
Never rains unless it pours.
Oh, my! What shall we do?
Oh, my! We'll get wet through.
Lucky fellers, with umbrellas
May manage to keep dry,
But still the rain keeps falling,
Falling, falling from the sky.

The storm continues to increase in violence as—

the CURTAIN *falls*

ACT II

SCENE 1

Outside the Inn

The tables and chairs outside the Inn have been removed, and Market stalls are set up RC *and up* LC.

When the CURTAIN *rises, a busy weekly Market is in progress.* MARKET-WOMEN *display among other wares, chickens, sausages, bacon, sucking-pigs, heart-shaped gingerbreads, daffodils, edelweiss, vegetables, peaches, apricots and cherries. Others are mingling with the crowd of* VILLAGERS, *one offering pipes, one offering postcards, etc., etc. During the opening singing,* JOSEPHA *enters from the Inn.* LEOPOLD *follows her on. He carries a shopping basket.*

ENTR'ACTE AND OPENING CHORUS No. 9

JOSEPHA, LEOPOLD *and* MARKET-WOMEN

MARKET-WOMEN. Come along now, who's a-buying?
All your needs we are supplying.
Here are lovely picture postcards,
Which are finer far than most cards.
Daffodils, the fairest going,
All a-blowing and a-growing.
Branches thick with crimson berries,
Peaches, apricots and cherries.
Come, buy our edelweiss,
At such a modest price.
Take your pick from all our barrows,
Beans and cabbages and marrows.
And for those who like to eat roots,
We've got turnips, too, and beetroots.

A MARKET-WOMAN *offers Josepha a trayful of pipes.*

JOSEPHA [*taking a pipe*] This meerschaum pipe,
It's just his type,
For Doctor Sutton, I will buy.
[*She hands the pipe to Leopold*]

LEOPOLD [*spoken; aside*] I hope he'll swallow it and die.

A MARKET-WOMAN *offers Josepha a tray of chocolates.*

JOSEPHA [*taking some chocolates*]·
These choc'lates, too, I'll take;
He won't despise them.

LEOPOLD [*spoken; aside*] I hope they choke him when he tries them.

A MARKET-WOMAN *offers Josepha a tray of gingerbread.*

JOSEPHA [*taking a gingerbread*]
This heart-shaped cake will be a token.

LEOPOLD [*spoken; aside*] Of all the faithful hearts you've broken.

JOSEPHA [*moving to the stall up* RC]
This chicken as well.
It looks right enough.
[*She hands the chicken to Leopold*]

WHITE HORSE INN — ACT II

LEOPOLD [*spoken; aside*] For our dear friend Herr Sutton it can't be too tough. [MUSIC]

JOSEPHA. And this sucking-pig, too,
Which I'm sure he would wish
To dine on next Sunday,
After the fish.
[*She hands the sucking-pig to Leopold*]

LEOPOLD [*spoken; aside*] Pig! A most suitable dish.

MARKET-WOMEN. Come along now, who's a-buying?
All your needs we are supplying.
Here are lovely picture postcards,
Which are finer far than most cards.
Daffodils, the fairest going,
All a-blowing and a-growing.
Branches thick with crimson berries,
Peaches, apricots and cherries.

During the final lines of the Chorus, the MARKET-WOMEN *and the* VILLAGERS *exit.*

Come, buy our edelweiss,
At such a modest price.
Take your pick from all our barrows,
Beans and cabbages and marrows.
And for those who like to eat roots,
We've got turnips, too, and beetroots.

LEOPOLD *looks crestfallen.*

JOSEPHA [*seeing Leopold's expression*] Anything the matter, Leopold?
LEOPOLD. Yes. [*He takes the pig from his basket*] I can't stand this pig. It reminds me of my Aunt Agatha.
JOSEPHA. It's for Herr Sutton's Sunday supper. Take it to the kitchen.
LEOPOLD. I'm a head waiter, not a messenger-boy. Certainly not a messenger of love. [*He puts the pig in his basket*]
JOSEPHA. So, you won't do as you're told.
LEOPOLD [*taking the heart-shaped gingerbread from his basket*] Not when I'm told something I won't do. [*He breaks the gingerbread in half*]
JOSEPHA. Have you thought seriously of what you're doing, Leopold?
LEOPOLD. Yes. And when Leopold says "yes", he means "yes". And when he says "no", he means "no". [*He puts the pieces of the gingerbread in the basket*]
JOSEPHA. Very well, then, you're discharged.
LEOPOLD. Good! [*He puts the basket on the ground*] You can do your own dirty work in future. You can look after Aunt Aggie.
JOSEPHA. Oh, indeed! [*She picks up the basket and moves towards the Inn door*] Good-bye, Leopold.
LEOPOLD [*stopping her*] Just a moment. Have you thought seriously of what you're doing, Josepha?
JOSEPHA. Yes. And when Josepha says "yes", she means "yes". And when she says "no"—you can go. [*She turns to go*]
LEOPOLD [*stopping her*] Take a last good look at me. You'll never see my like again. I go, never to return.

JOSEPHA *does not react.*

I repeat—never to return.
JOSEPHA. *Bon voyage.*
LEOPOLD. If I leave now, remember, I shan't ever come back, not even if you go on your knees and beg me to.
JOSEPHA. There's not much danger of that.
LEOPOLD. Wait and see. Good-bye. We meet no more.

JOSEPHA. I'm delighted to hear it. Where are you going?
LEOPOLD. Somewhere where I'm wanted—where I'm appreciated—where the wide open spaces beckon me; where I can hear the call of the sea.
JOSEPHA. As a stowaway, or just an ordinary sailor?
LEOPOLD. As an able-bodied seaman, of course.
JOSEPHA. What makes you think you're able-bodied? I've never seen any signs of it.
LEOPOLD. When I'm serving in my country's navy you'll be sorry for those harsh words.
JOSEPHA. The Swiss haven't got a navy.
LEOPOLD. Oh. Haven't they? Then I'll enlist in the Legion.
JOSEPHA. The Foreign Legion? You? How utterly absurd!
LEOPOLD [*with emotion*] The Legion—that company of broken men who, in the great open spaces, find their souls anew.
JOSEPHA. Don't make me laugh.

JOSEPHA exits to the Inn, laughing.

" GOOD-BYE "

No. 10

LEOPOLD *and* MEN

LEOPOLD [*speaking over the music*] She laughs while hearts are breaking.

A bugle calls.

Hark! The bugle call. [*He sings*]

My heart is broken,
But what care I?
Such pride inside may be woken,
I'll try my best not to cry,
By and by,
When the final farewells must be spoken.
I'll join the Legion,
That's what I'll do.
And in some far distant region,
Where human hearts are staunch and true,
I shall start my life anew.

Good-bye, it's time
I sought a foreign clime,
Where I may find
There are hearts more kind
Than I leave behind.
And so, I go
To fight a savage foe,
Although I know
I'll be sometimes missed by the girls I've kissed.

In some Abyssinian French Dominion
I shall do my bit,
And fall for the flag if I must.
Where the desert sand is nice and handy,
I'll be full of grit;
You won't see my heels for the dust.
I'll do or die.
You'll know the reason why
When told of bold Leopold's " last stand "
For the Fatherland.

The WAITERS *and other* MEN *have entered, for speciality routine.*   MUSIC

  Good-bye. Good-bye.
  I wish you all a last Good-bye.
  Good-bye. Good-bye.
  I wish you all a last Good-bye.

MEN. Good-bye. Good-bye. Good-bye.
  Good-bye. Good-bye. Good-bye.

LEOPOLD. I'm sick of standing
  Behind a chair
  Bread-sauce respectfully handing.
  Henceforth I'm free as the air,
  I declare,
  And my chest has a chance of expanding.
  I've done with women,
  And now I plan
  To join the army of he-men.
  And show the ladies, if I can,
  That a waiter's still a man.

ALL. Good-bye, it's time,
  I sought a foreign clime,
  Where I may find
  There are hearts more kind
  Than I leave behind.
  And so, I go
  To fight a savage foe,
  Although I know
  I'll be sometimes missed by the girls I've kissed.
  In some Abyssinian French Dominion
  I shall do my bit,
  And fall for the flag if I must
  Where the desert sand is nice and handy,
  I'll be full of grit;
  You won't see my heels for the dust.

  I'll do or die,
  You'll know the reason why
  When told of bold Leopold's " last stand "
  For the Fatherland.
  Good-bye. Good-bye.
  I wish you all a last Good-bye.
  Good-bye. Good-bye.
  I wish you all a last Good-bye.

     EXIT MUSIC   No. 10a
   All exit, singing as they go. LEOPOLD *exits* R.

ALL. Good-bye. Good-bye.
  I wish you all a last Good-bye.
  Good-bye. Good-bye.
  I wish you all a last Good-bye.
     LEOPOLD *re-enters* R.
    KARL *runs on from the Inn.*

KARL. Herr Leopold! Is it true? You're leaving?
LEOPOLD. Well, you know, men with ambition cannot resist getting better jobs. And now let me give you my last will and testament.
KARL [weeping] Yes, Herr Leopold.
LEOPOLD. Take particular care of the honeymoon couple in number thirty-six. After knocking at the door, always count five before entering. On wet days count eight. See that the bridegroom has plenty of good nourishing food, lobsters, celery, oysters and caviare. Administer aspirin every two hours to the bride.
KARL [weeping bitterly] Yes, Herr Leopold.
LEOPOLD. And remember, above all, a waiter is also a *man*.

KARL *and* LEOPOLD *fall weeping on each other's necks.*

JOSEPHA *enters from the Inn.*

JOSEPHA. What's all this howling about? Stop snivelling at once.
LEOPOLD. I'm not snivelling. I'm laughing.

LEOPOLD, *howling, exits down* L.

JOSEPHA [*to Karl*] And you, you little idiot, what are *you* howling about?
KARL. I'm not howling—I'm laughing.

KARL *exits to the Inn.*

JOSEPHA. These servants!

SUTTON *enters on the balcony* L.

SUTTON. Good morning, Josepha.
JOSEPHA. Ah, Herr Sutton. Slept well?
SUTTON. Thank you. Very well indeed.

OTTOLINE, *unseen by* JOSEPHA, *enters down* R. SUTTON *sees Ottoline and directs his conversation to her.*

What a view! What lovely things one sees from this balcony.
JOSEPHA. Always so charming.
SUTTON [*to Ottoline*] I'll join you in a moment.
JOSEPHA [*thinking it is she who is being addressed*] There's no need—I'll bring your breakfast upstairs.
SUTTON [*to Ottoline*] I want so much to speak to you.

SUTTON *exits from the balcony.*

JOSEPHA [*delighted*] Do you? I am glad. [*She moves to the Inn door*] I'll cook it myself—fried herring—marmalade—scrambled eggs—toast—coffee . . .

JOSEPHA *exits quickly down* L.

SUTTON *enters from the Inn.*

OTTOLINE. Well, Mr Counsel for the Prosecution. And what is it you want to say to me, so particularly?
SUTTON [*taking her hand*] Ottoline . . .
OTTOLINE. Don't be silly, you know papa can't bear the sight of you.
SUTTON. Papa! By tonight he'll be giving me instructions never to let you out of my sight.
OTTOLINE. Are you a magician?
SUTTON. I'm a solicitor, anyhow. I'll get round him. [*He puts his arm around her*] Ottoline— you're the only girl I ever loved.
OTTOLINE. Are you trying to get round *me*, too?

"YOU, TOO"

SUTTON, OTTOLINE and DANCERS

SUTTON.
Poets have written that love cannot die,
Yet, if once bitten, one's apt to be shy.
Girls are delicious,
Yet they're capricious,
That's what makes me so suspicious.

OTTOLINE.
Love is a fever that lasts but a day,
Man's a deceiver, so fickle and gay,
He'll kiss a miss,
And ride away, they say.
You, too,
When you're old
May grow cold and untrue. You, too.

SUTTON.
You, too,
May ignore
What you swore you would do. You, too.

OTTOLINE.
I pray
That each vow
Taken now, love will hold you to.

SUTTON.
And say:
"Won't you share
Joy and care
All life through,

BOTH.
You two?"

The DANCERS *enter and dance until the end of the number.*

OTTOLINE.
Love, says the poet, can never be lost,
Yet, as we know it,
Alas to our cost,
Love so intensive,
Can be expensive,
That's why I feel apprehensive.

SUTTON.
Friendships may falter
As all will agree,
Hearts too may alter
And long to be free.
Yet time shall bring
No change to me, you'll see.

BOTH.
You, too,
When you're old
May grow cold and untrue. You, too.
You, too,
May ignore, etc.

I pray
That each vow
Taken now, love will hold you to.

Scene 1 — WHITE HORSE INN

And say:
"Won't you share
Joy and care
All life through,
You two, you two?"

EXIT MUSIC   No. 11a

The DANCERS *exit.*

SUTTON *and* OTTOLINE *exit down* R.

GRINKLE *enters from the Inn. He is dressed in a complete Tyrolean outfit. He presents a comical picture and looks at himself with disgust.*

GRINKLE. Eeh, I do feel a proper twerp in this fancy outfit. If they were to see me like this in Oldham I should be drummed out of t'Oddfellows. [*He calls*] Hey, waiter! Waiter, where are you?

LEOPOLD *enters from the Inn. He is now dressed in a very smart Tyrolean costume and is smoking a cigarette in a long holder.*

Ah, there you are.
LEOPOLD [*airily*] Terribly sorry, my dear friend, but I'm not waiting any more.
GRINKLE. What *are* you, then?
LEOPOLD. A gentleman of leisure.
GRINKLE. Nonsense! Bring me my breakfast.

JOSEPHA *enters from the Inn.*

LEOPOLD. Sorry, but I'm afraid you'll have to bring it yourself, and while you're about it you might as well bring mine, too.
GRINKLE. The man's off his onion.
JOSEPHA. Please pay no attention to Leopold. He's discharged.
LEOPOLD [*to Grinkle*] Who is this woman? I seem to have seen her face before. [*He crosses with a comedy walk to* R] So long! I'm going down the town to give the girls a treat.
JOSEPHA. *What* are you going to do?
LEOPOLD. Show the civilized world that Leopold has sex-appeal.

LEOPOLD, *continuing the comedy walk, exits down* R.

GRINKLE. Eeh! A nice state of things. I ask for my breakfast and all I get is a large portion of self-appointed sex-appeal.
JOSEPHA. Didn't you have a good night?
GRINKLE. Good? Young woman, have you ever tried sleeping in a pigeon-loft?
JOSEPHA. We were full up...
GRINKLE. And I'm *fed* up. Oh—[*ecstatically*] when I remember that lovely bed-sitting room in Clacton. The floral linoleum on the floor. The jug and basin on the marble wash-stand—and the whatnot in the how-d'ye-do to match. [*He smiles*]
JOSEPHA. There now, how charming you can be. When you smile you're not at all bad-looking.
GRINKLE [*flattered*] Do you really think so?

JOSEPHA *tickles Grinkle under his chin.*

[*He changes his tune*] Here! Here! No compliments. I shall be finding them on my bill. [*He crosses to* L]
JOSEPHA. There you go again! Grumble! Grumble! And the world so beautiful all around you.

"IN SALZKAMMERGUT"

MUSIC No. 12

JOSEPHA, GRINKLE, CHORUS *and* DANCERS

JOSEPHA. Storm clouds have fled,
And in their stead
Swallows circle in the air above.
Bright shines the sun,
Now ev'ry one
Suddenly becomes aware of love.
Here girls and boys
Taste of its joys,
Where a hundred hearts are lost and won.
Well do they know
Where they must go,
If they want a bit of fun.

In Salzkammergut, Salzkammergut,
Come what may,
Life's as bright and gay
As can be.
There's joy to be found
All Summer round,
Night and day.
That's the time for play,
You'll agree.
There's happiness there;
You can banish trouble and care,
Finding fun and laughter where'er you may go.
For there in the Spring
Young lovers bring
Songs to sing.
And you hear them yodelling,
Holdrio.

The CHORUS, *in Tyrolean costume, enter during the following verse.*

Now for a dance,
Here comes your chance
If there's any likely lad about,
He'll trip it now,
Lightly, I vow,
With the maiden whom he's mad about.
Come, have a try.
Come, don't be shy.
Dancing's an extremely useful art.
That you can prove
Later, when you've
Danc'd your way into her heart.

ALL. In Salzkammergut, Salzkammergut,
Come what may,
Life's as bright and gay
As can be.
There's joy to be found
All Summer round,
Night and day.

That's the time for play,
You'll agree.
There's happiness there;
You can banish trouble and care,
Finding fun and laughter where'er you may go.
For there in the Spring
Young lovers bring
Songs to sing.
And you hear them yodelling,
Holdrio.

The DANCERS *enter and dance.*

GRINKLE. Dancing in shorts
At health resorts
Ain't a sport I'm very keen upon.
I'd sooner take
Part in a " wake ",
With a gradely lass to lean upon.
These foreign spas!
No Public Bars!
Nowt but dizzy Alpine heights to climb.
I'd sooner spend
Lent at Southend.
Give me Margate ev'ry time.

Or Clacton-on-Sea. Clacton-on-Sea.
There I'd dwell
And I'd feel as well
As could be.
This thin mountain air
It can't compare
With the smell
When the *Clacton Belle*
Puts to sea.
It's lovely out here.
But I miss the shrimps and the Pier,
But I find no " kick " in the beer,
It's all foam.
And so, the next time,
If ever I'm
Asked to sing,
You will hear me yodelling:
" Home, Sweet. Home ".

KATHI *enters and yodels, while the* CHORUS *harmonize.*

KATHI. Holdrio-drio. Holdrio-drio.
Holdrio. Holdrio-drio.
Holdrio-drio. Holdrio.
Oh—oh.
CHORUS. Ah.

All dance and exit except GRINKLE, *who is left alone on the stage, practising Tyrolean steps. The music continues softly.*

MELOS

OTTOLINE *enters down* R.

OTTOLINE [*over the music*] Daddy!
GRINKLE. Guten Morgen, meine Maderl.
OTTOLINE. Guten morgen, Herr Grinkle.

OTTOLINE *and* GRINKLE *do a little stepping dance together.*

GRINKLE. Nothing can upset me today.

KARL *enters from the Inn. He carries a visiting card.*

KARL [*crossing to Grinkle*] A gentleman to see you, sir. [*He hands the card to Grinkle*]

The music fades.

GRINKLE. What's this? [*He reads the card*] " Smith, Hammersmith." [*He rages*] The old crook! [*To Ottoline*] The Opposition has arrived.
OTTOLINE. The one who buttons up the back? The old scoundrel!
GRINKLE [*to Karl*] Show him in.

KARL *exits to the Inn.*

OTTOLINE. And show him *up*, too, Daddy.
GRINKLE [*rolling up his sleeves*] I'll teach the old blood-sucker . . . [*He advances threateningly towards the Inn door*]

SIGISMUND SMITH *enters from the Inn. He is a very smart and dapper young man, with a bald head, which is now covered by a beret.*

SIGISMUND. How do you do?
GRINKLE. What? *You* are " Shirtopants "?
SIGISMUND. It was really my father's invention.
GRINKLE. I see. A chip off the old block, eh?
SIGISMUND. Just a splinter. May I introduce myself? Sigismund Smith, Underwear, of Hammersmith—you may have heard of me. I've heard of you, Mr Grinkle. You see, my father so often told me what a remarkable man you are, and how I oughtn't to miss seeing you. " See Grinkle and die ", he often said to me. And now, when I see you in the flesh, in that very slimming costume, I confess I wouldn't mind dying.
GRINKLE. You're a fine outspoken young chap. [*He pats Sigismund's cheek then suddenly slaps it hard*] What made you think you could take me in? [*To Ottoline*] Look at this tailor's dummy. [*To Sigismund*] Could anyone possibly propose him for membership of [*local*] Golf Club?

GRINKLE *and* OTTOLINE *exit to the Inn.*

SIGISMUND. Was he just being funny? Or is he angry with me? Jealous of my looks, perhaps.

" SIGISMUND "

SIGISMUND, CHORUS and DANCERS

SIGISMUND. When Sigismund was born the neighbours flocked for many a mile,
To see his angel-smile;
They thought it well worth while.
Today his charm
Still spreads alarm.
He seems by nature planned
To be a man
No woman can
Withstand.

SCENE 1   WHITE HORSE INN

" Oh, Sigismund," they cry, " we're vanquished by your beauty.
And yet what harm that fatal charm of yours can do.
It makes us wives lead double lives and shirk our duty;
We leave our houses and our spouses just for you.
Tho' other men we now and then may bill and coo with,
We're bound to own 'tis you alone we're mad about,
There may perhaps be lesser chaps that we can do with,
But you're the man we simply cannot do without."

The spinster who meets Sigismund on Sunday afternoons,
Her eyes grow like balloons,
She generally swoons.
He can't conceal
The sex-appeal
Which fascinates them all,
For he's a chap
For whom the flappers fall.

" Oh, Sigismund," they sigh, " we're dazzled by your beauty.
For tho' in books we've read of looks like yours, it's true.
The wicked Earl may ask a girl to be his ' cutie ',
But as a snare he can't compare at all with you.
The simple souls for moonlight strolls we girls have gone with
Would never dare to take the air when you're about.
You may suppose we've other beaux we can get on with;
But you're the only one we can't get on without,
But you're the only one we can't get on without."

The music continues. SIGISMUND *exits* R *then re-enters with the* CHORUS *and the* GIRL TYROLEAN DANCERS *for a burlesque tango*

CHORUS.   " Oh, Sigismund," they cry, " we're vanquished by your beauty.
We're bound to own 'tis you alone we're mad about.
It makes the wives lead double lives and shirk their duty,
But you're the man they simply cannot do without,
But you're the only one they can't get on without."

The CHORUS *and* DANCERS *exit.*

PROFESSOR HINZEL *and his daughter* GRETEL, *and* JOSEPHA *enter from the Inn.* HINZEL *is a kindly old idealist. He carries a small bag.*

SIGISMUND. Well, well, if it isn't my old friend, Professor Hinzel. [*To Josepha*] We met in the train.
HINZEL [*to Josepha*] This gentleman was very attentive to me—and to my daughter. Wasn't he, my dear ?
GRETEL. Yes, Papa.
HINZEL. By the way, do your terms include breakfast ?
JOSEPHA. No. Only service and light.
HINZEL. Ah, we can wait on ourselves, can't we, Gretel ? And we've brought our own light. [*He opens his bag and takes out a candle*] So could we have breakfast in lieu of service and light ? Let me see how much of our travelling fund we've got left. [*He counts his money*]
SIGISMUND [*aside to Josepha*] Charge them half price. I'll settle the other half.

JOSEPHA *gives an understanding nod.*

JOSEPHA [*to Hinzel*] The charge for a room, including board and bath, is ten kronen a day.
HINZEL. A lot of money. But still, I suppose we must accept.

SIGISMUND *smiles.*

Don't laugh, young man. It's not so easy nowadays for a schoolmaster to travel about, is it, Gretel ?

GRETEL. Nein, Papa.
HINZEL. Every third summer we go abroad together, Gretel and I.
JOSEPHA. And how do you spend the other two?
HINZEL. One, remembering where we've been the year before and the other looking forward to where we're going next year. Ah. Foreign travel! How I love it. Those little mountain railways. Up she goes. Up she goes. Up, up, up. Up she goes. [*He gets carried away by the thought, imitates the sound of an engine and goes around the stage " playing trains "*]

The others become infected and follow Hinzel around " playing trains " and saying " Up she goes ", etc., until GRETEL *stops them.*

GRETEL. Papa!
HINZEL. Yes, I know. I'm talking too much. I'll climb up and inspect our little nest under the roof.
JOSEPHA. This way.

HINZEL, *imitating a train and saying " Up she goes ", exits to the Inn.*

JOSEPHA, *laughing, follows Hinzel off.*

SIGISMUND. Would you like me to show you the sights? Or are you afraid to trust yourself to me?
GRETEL [*shyly*] Oh, no.
SIGISMUND. Come along, then.

DANCE   No. 13a

SIGISMUND *and* GRETEL

SIGISMUND *and* GRETEL *at the end of their eccentric dance exit up* R.

GRINKLE *enters from the Inn.*

SUTTON *enters down* R.

SUTTON. Ah, Mr Grinkle. I want to speak to you about your law-suit.
GRINKLE. Law-suit? I'm out here for pleasure—*my* pleasure, not yours. Not a word about the law-suit. [*He pauses*] How's it going?
SUTTON. I've advised old Smith to settle out of court.
GRINKLE. Impossible! I refuse. [*He pauses*] What's he prepared to pay?
SUTTON. That entirely depends on me.
GRINKLE. On *you?* I depend on you? I'd sooner button up the back.
SUTTON. But, Mr Grinkle . . .
GRINKLE [*interrupting*] You can't get round me, young man. Let's get this straight. From now on I don't know you, and you don't know me. As far as I'm concerned we're strangers—understand?
SUTTON. Very well. I've never even met you.
GRINKLE. That's right. And I've never met you, and I don't want to. Good morning. [*He turns his back to Sutton*]
SUTTON. Good afternoon. [*He turns his back to Grinkle*]

KATHI, *happily yodelling to herself, enters up* R.

KATHI. Herr Grinkle. I have a registered letter here for Herr Grinkle.
GRINKLE. That's right. Give it to me.
KATHI. Oh, no, Herr Grinkle. That wouldn't be correct. I must know, first of all, that you are Herr Grinkle.
GRINKLE. But, good Heavens! I *am* Herr Grinkle. You know I am.
KATHI. I know, of course. But officially I don't know anything. I've got no proof.
GRINKLE. You don't expect me to go mountaineering with a visiting-card in my pocket.
KATHI. Of course, if you could get someone to identify you. [*She looks at Sutton*] Ah, what about Herr Sutton? [*To Sutton*] Do you know this gentleman?
SUTTON. Which gentleman? [*He looks at Grinkle*] Oh, that? Sorry. I don't know him.

SCENE 1   WHITE HORSE INN

GRINKLE [*angrily*] What?
SUTTON. We're strangers. We've never even met one another.
GRINKLE. Ah! You don't know me, don't you?
SUTTON [*airily*] No. I knew a Herr Grinkle once. A stout, rather tiresome man with a rotten temper. I'm glad to say I've entirely forgotten him.
GRINKLE. Is that so? You . . . [*He vacillates between his annoyance and a desire to get the registered letter. After a moment's hesitation, he goes to Sutton, takes off his hat and bows*] Perhaps you'll allow me to introduce myself—Grinkle of Oldham—Underwear.
SUTTON. Delighted, I'm sure. My name's Sutton, of Sutton, Sutton, Sutton and Sutton. [*He shakes hands with Grinkle*] Lovely weather for the time of year, eh? [*To Kathi*] This is my dear old friend, Mr Grinkle of Oldham. A charming fellow. He buttons up the front.

                              KATHI *gives the letter to Grinkle.*

GRINKLE. Thank you. [*He chucks Kathi under her chin*]

                            KATHI *smiles at Grinkle, and exits down L.*

That's the first time I ever got off with a postman. [*He opens the letter*] It's from that old scoundrel Smith. [*He reads*] "Herewith my son, Sigismund, forwarded to you on appro as per Messrs Suttons' request." [*He looks at Sutton*] Your request?
SUTTON. Yes. It occurred to me that this young man and your daughter . . .
GRINKLE. Oh. So that's what you meant by settling out of court, is it? A marriage settlement?
SUTTON. Exactly.
GRINKLE. Impossible!
SUTTON. Why? He's a millionaire, you know.
GRINKLE. He is? Yes. Oh, well, that makes it a little less impossible.
SUTTON. If the firms of Grinkle and Smith could amalgamate they'd corner the underwear of the world.
GRINKLE. What a "combination". We could compromise and button up at t'side.
SUTTON. That certainly would be compromising.
GRINKLE. Ah, but you don't know my daughter. She's so obstinate.
SUTTON. I might be able to persuade her. As a lawyer, you know . . .
GRINKLE. She wouldn't listen.
SUTTON. I could try to make her. If you agree.
GRINKLE. My dear young friend, of course I agree. Don't leave her side until you have her safely married.
SUTTON. I can guarantee satisfaction. I won't leave a stone unturned until I get what I want.
GRINKLE. Do you know, young man, I'm just beginning to like you.

                                    BALLET   No. 14

                                "SALZKAMMERGUT"

                   SUTTON, GRINKLE, KATHI, CHORUS *and* DANCERS

SUTTON.   In Salzkammergut, Salzkammergut,
                     Day and night,
                     Life's as gay and bright
                     As can be.
GRINKLE.   A feast we'll prepare.
                     Ev'ryone there
                     We'll invite,
                     And we'll all get tight
                     After tea.

SUTTON.	With bridegroom and bride When the fatal knot then is tied To the village church with what pride You will go.	MUSIC

The full CHORUS *of* TYROLEANS *and the* DANCERS *enter during the following verse.*

GRINKLE. The welkin will ring
Like *anything*
When I sing.
And if I start yodelling—
" Holdrio ".

A big national dance follows.

KATHI *enters, and yodels and sings during the dance, while the* CHORUS *harmonize.*

KATHI. Holdrio, holdrio, holdrio.
On meadow and lake
At the dawn of the day,
The shadows awake
And creep swiftly away.
O'er valley and hill
Not an echo is stirred,
All's peaceful and still,
Not a sound to be heard.
Holdrio-drio, holdrio-drio, holdrio.

The dance continues.

ALL. In Salzkammergut, Salzkammergut,
Come what may,
Life's as bright and gay as can be.
There's joy to be found
All Summer round,
Night and day.
That's the time for play, you'll agree.
There's happiness there ;
You can banish trouble and care,
Finding fun and laughter
Where'er you may go.
For there in the Spring
Young lovers bring
Songs to sing.
And you hear them yodelling,
Holdrio.

The number ends with a picture.
The lights dim to BLACK-OUT *as—*

LIGHTING CUE 7

the RUNNING TABS *close*

SCENE 2
The Pine Wood

The setting is a front cloth depicting a Pine Wood. There is a rustic bench C.
When the RUNNING TABS *open,* SIGISMUND *and* GRETEL *are seated on the bench,* GRETEL R *of Sigismund.*

SIGISMUND. Well, little chatterbox, here we are.

GRETEL [*dumbly*] Ya.
SIGISMUND [*forcing the conversation*] It's nice in the forest, isn't it?
GRETEL. Ya.
SIGISMUND [*after a pause*] The trees are rather green for the time of the year.
GRETEL. Oh, ya.
SIGISMUND [*amorously*] Isn't it time we made some headway?
GRETEL. Oh, no.
SIGISMUND. Do you never say anything but "Oh, ya" and "Oh, no"? It makes conversation rather difficult. Say, "Oh, no, Sigismund" just once.
GRETEL. Oh, no.
SIGISMUND. Why not? It's such a nice name, and commits you to nothing.
GRETEL. Oh, no.
SIGISMUND. Come on—say it—try. [*Coaxingly*] "Sigismund."
GRETEL. I can't.
SIGISMUND [*rising*] Be careful, I can be very cross when I like. [*He turns to go*]
GRETEL. Wait. I'll tell you why I can't. I—I . . . [*She hesitates*]
SIGISMUND. Go on. Go on. [*He resumes his seat*]
GRETEL [*lisping*] You *th*ee, I li*th*p. And *Th*igi*th*mund ha*th* got *th*o many e*th*-e*th*.
SIGISMUND. You li*th*p—I mean lisp? But it's charming. I should love to hear you sing: "I *th*aw E*th*aw *th*itting on a *th*ee-*th*aw."
GRETEL. You're laughing at me. All laugh at me. But they're funny enough them*th*elves.
SIGISMUND. *Th*o you *th*ay.
GRETEL. For in*th*tan*th*, if you *th*aw a young man with a bald head, you'd laugh your*th*elf *th*ick.
SIGISMUND. I don't know if I would—because you see, I—I . . . [*He hesitates*]
GRETEL. Go on. Go on.
SIGISMUND. Well—you see. [*He removes his beret revealing his bald head*]

GRETEL *laughs.*

GRETEL [*controlling herself*] But it *th*uits you *th*o well.
SIGISMUND. Do you think so?
GRETEL. Ye*th*. Now we are quit*th*.
SIGISMUND. What a load you've taken off my mind. I feel ten years younger.
GRETEL. My bald-headed boy.
SIGISMUND. My sweet little lisping pixie-wixie.
GRETEL. What's a pick*th*y-wick*th*y?

"FAIRIES" No. 15

SIGISMUND *and* GRETEL

They rise and move down C.

SIGISMUND. Tell me you believe that there are fairies about,
For there is no doubt
It's true.
GRETEL. I believe it, indeed I do.
More than ever since I met you.
SIGISMUND. If, instead of looking like a shell-fish, you got
More elfish, and not so bland,
I would lead you to where
We could live upon air
In some wonderful fairyland.
If we were fairies, me and you,
We'd do what fairies always do:
I'd write you an epistle,
And post it in a thistle.

		MUSIC
GRETEL.	I'd wear a daisy for a hat.	
SIGISMUND.	You'd look extremely well in that.	
BOTH.	We'd dance all night, from dark till dawn, With the fairies on the lawn.	
GRETEL.	Side by side, we'd sit upon a mushroom, we two.	
SIGISMUND.	With just room for you And me.	
GRETEL.	We'd have honey each night for tea.	
SIGISMUND.	'Twould be funny to keep a bee.	
GRETEL.	Ev'ry night within a foxglove petal I'd creep And settle to sleep No doubt.	
SIGISMUND.	If I climbed up the stalk, How the neighbours would talk. They would think we were walking out.	

The RUNNING TABS *close behind Sigismund and Gretel*

BOTH.	If we were fairies, me and you, We'd do as fairies always do :
SIGISMUND.	We'd harness up our squirrel And drive across the Tyrol.
GRETEL.	A nut would be the hut we'd share.
SIGISMUND.	I hope the " kernel " won't be there.
BOTH.	But, if he is, we'll dance till dawn, With the fairies on the lawn.

GRETEL *and* SIGISMUND *do a short eccentric dance.*

We'll dance all night from dark till dawn,
With the fairies on the lawn.

GRETEL *and* SIGISMUND *exit* R.
KATHI, *yodelling as usual, enters* L.
KARL *enters* R.

KARL. Hullo, Kathi. Still singing? Been breakfasting off bird-seed as usual?
KATHI. None of your impertinence, young man. Where's Leopold?
KARL. Haven't you heard—poor Leopold's got the sack. What do you want him for, anyway?
KATHI. I don't want him but he's wanted at the Town Hall. There's a meeting of the Parish Council and I was told to find him.
KARL. Well, I expect you'll find him at the nearest bar—drinking himself slowly but painlessly to death. Good luck.

KARL *exits* L.
KATHI, *yodelling, follows him off as—*

the lights BLACK-OUT

LIGHTING CUE 8

CHANGE OF SCENE MUSIC   No. 15a

SCENE 3

The Town Hall

The setting is a front-cloth depicting the interior of the Town Hall. There is a long table across the stage C *set with chairs behind it and one chair at the right end.*

When the RUNNING TABS *open, the* COUNCILLORS *are seated above the table, with the local* MAYOR *in the centre. Two*

SCENE 3 — WHITE HORSE INN

or three of the COUNCILLORS *have long beards. The* LADY SECRETARY *is seated at the right end of the table. She is a gaunt female, wearing spectacles. There is a great noise of talk and chatter, which is at last put to an end by the* MAYOR *who rings his hand-bell and thumps on the table. The music fades.*

MAYOR. Order, please! I will now ask the Secretary to read the Minutes of the last Meeting.

> *The* SECRETARY *rises and reads in a high-pitched voice. As she does so, the* COUNCILLORS *talk and chatter to one another so loudly that hardly any words of hers are heard.*

SECRETARY [*reading*] " At a meeting of the Parish Council held on Thursday the seventh of May, His Worship the Mayor, in the chair—the Minutes of the last meeting were read and confirmed."

> *The* MAYOR *rings his bell and a momentary silence ensues.*

MAYOR. Order, please! Is it your pleasure, gentlemen, that we take the Minutes as read?

> *The* COUNCILLORS *murmur assent. The* SECRETARY *resumes her seat.*

Good. We can now proceed to the business of the day. As you are all aware, His Imperial Majesty has graciously signified his intention of paying us a visit today——
COUNCILLORS [*ad lib.*] Hear! Hear!
MAYOR. —in order to be present at the opening of the shooting season.
COUNCILLORS [*ad lib.*] Hear! Hear!
1ST COUNCILLOR [*anxiously*] Will he come *here*, your Worship?
MAYOR. He may. And in case he does, I have taken the responsibility of composing a brief address of welcome. It is in verse. [*He rises and clears his throat*]

> " All hail, Imperial Eagle!
> Each loyal heart today,
> High-soaring like a seagull
> And faithful as a beagle,
> Shall welcome you and say:
> ' Hurrah! Hurrah! Hooray! ' "

> *The* COUNCILLORS *applaud.*

[*He resumes his seat*] Thank you. [*He pauses*] Now, we will imagine that His Majesty comes in by —[*he points* L] that door over there. [*He rises*] We all rise to our feet——

> *The* COUNCILLORS *rise.*

—and at a given signal from me—one, two, three . . .
ALL. All hail, Imperial Eagle!
Each loyal heart today,

> LEOPOLD *enters* L. *He is slightly intoxicated.*

High-soaring like a seagull
And faithful as a beagle,
Shall welcome you and say:
" Hurrah! Hurrah! Hooray! "
LEOPOLD [*raising his hat*] Thank you for your kind reshception. [*He moves to the left end of the table*] Three cheers for the jolly old seagull—and hooray for the jolly old beagle. [*He falls over the table and crawls along it to the far end. As he looks up he comes face to face with the Secretary and collapses on the floor*]

> *The* COUNCILLORS *are indignant at Leopold's behaviour, protest and resume their seats.*

MAYOR. Herr Leopold! I'm ashamed of you. Sit down at once.
LEOPOLD [*on the floor*] What the devil do you think I'm doing?
MAYOR. Don't you realize that the Emperor is coming here?
LEOPOLD. Emperor? Which Emperor?
MAYOR. *Our* Emperor, of course.

LEOPOLD *pulls himself together, rises, stands to attention and salutes.* MUSIC

LEOPOLD. The Emperor! Why didn't you say so before?
MAYOR. I did. You wouldn't listen.
LEOPOLD. And where will His Majesty stay?
2ND COUNCILLOR. At the *Blue Dragon*, of course.
3RD COUNCILLOR. No! At the *Palace Hotel*.
4TH COUNCILLOR. Nonsense! At the *Esplanade*.
OTHER COUNCILLORS [*ad lib.*] The *Alpine Rose, Mountview*, etc.
MAYOR [*ringing his bell*] Order! Order!
LEOPOLD [*still a little tipsy*] Lady and gentlemen, you're all talking nonsense. There's only one place he can stay at—the *White Horse Inn*. It's the only hotel in town with a bathroom, complete with " shower " and hot and cold and usual offices. You can't expect the Emperor to walk to the bottom of the garden every time he wants to wash his hands.

The COUNCILLORS *protest.*

[*He takes the Mayor's bell and rings it*] Order! Please! The resolution before the Council is that His Majesty be invited to put up at the *White Horse Inn.* Those in favour say " Aye ".
ALL. No.
LEOPOLD. The " Ayes " have it. Carried unanimously.
1ST COUNCILLOR. Never! Who are *you* to take the Chair? You're only a waiter.
LEOPOLD. What did you say? *Only* a waiter?

FIGHT MUSIC   No. 15b

LEOPOLD *gives the 1st Councillor a terrific box on the ear which starts a free fight among the* COUNCILLORS, *ending with* LEOPOLD *falling over the* SECRETARY *who falls backward on her chair, revealing her long red-flannel bloomers.*

The lights BLACK-OUT *as—*

LIGHTING CUE 9

the RUNNING TABS *close*

The music continues.

The lights come up.

LIGHTING CUE 10

LEOPOLD *rushes on* R *in front of the* RUNNING TABS, *frantically chased by the* COUNCILLORS. *At the end of the line, the* MAYOR *tears across ringing his bell, followed by the* SECRETARY *holding up her skirts.* ALL *exit* L.

SCENE 4

The cow-shed

The cows are not used in this scene. It is assumed they are out grazing.

When the RUNNING TABS *open,* LEOPOLD *enters* L. *He is clutching the lower part of his back where he has been belaboured.* JOSEPHA *enters* R. *She has her sleeves rolled up. The music fades.*

JOSEPHA. What's the matter now?
LEOPOLD. Josepha! Have you heard the news?
JOSEPHA. I've been too busy to hear anything. I thought I'd discharged you.
LEOPOLD. So you did. All is over between us. I've nothing more to say to you—except the Emperor is coming today to open the shooting season, and he's going to stay at the *White Horse*.

SCENE 4 — WHITE HORSE INN

JOSEPHA [*agitated*]   The Emperor? Coming to open the *White Horse* and stay at the shooting season?   **MUSIC**
LEOPOLD.   Yes. I thought you'd like to know. Good morning. [*He turns to go*]
JOSEPHA.   Stop!
                        LEOPOLD *stops and turns.*
Good Heavens! But I don't know anything about Emperors.
LEOPOLD.   That's *your* trouble. Good morning. [*He turns to go*]
JOSEPHA.   Don't go, Leopold. Leopold! Don't go! Listen!
                        LEOPOLD *stops and turns.*
Who's going to wait on him if you go away?
LEOPOLD.   Oh, Herr Sutton will attend to all that. He's a very clever man. He'll manage. Good afternoon.
JOSEPHA [*imploringly*]   Leopold! Haven't you any feelings?
LEOPOLD.   Not any more.
JOSEPHA [*seductively*]   Leopold! *Dear* Leopold. Darling Leopold. Please. Please don't go.
                        LEOPOLD *starts to weaken then controls himself.*
LEOPOLD.   Steady, Leopold. [*He suddenly crosses to* L]   Good night.
JOSEPHA [*changing her tone; loudly*]   Good Heavens! Must I go on my knees and beg you to stay?
LEOPOLD [*stopping and turning*]   Certainly.
JOSEPHA.   You can't mean it. You can't be so cruel.
LEOPOLD [*moving* LC]   I can. On the knee. The floor has been scrubbed.
JOSEPHA.   But—Leopold . . .
LEOPOLD.   All right. If you won't . . . [*He turns to go*]
JOSEPHA.   Leopold! [*She drops to her knees*]   There!
                        LEOPOLD *triumphantly approaches* JOSEPHA *who lets her head fall on to her breast and puts her hands behind her in an attitude of complete surrender.*
LEOPOLD.   Now for my condition. Number One A: Herr Sutton leaves the hotel at once.
JOSEPHA.   What? [*She starts to rise*]
LEOPOLD.   Down!
                        JOSEPHA *drops.*
His Majesty will have the Balcony room, Number four.
JOSEPHA [*hesitating*]   I don't see how I can . . . [*She starts to rise*]
LEOPOLD.   Very well then. [*He turns to go*]
                        JOSEPHA *drops quickly.*
Is it agreed?
JOSEPHA [*rising; half laughing*]   You're so masterful. I never noticed it before.
LEOPOLD.   Masterful! That's me! [*He slaps his chest and coughs*]   And now go and change into your Sunday frock. The one I'm so sweet on. And directly I've finished my speech to the Emperor, you must escort him into the hotel.

CHANGE OF SCENE MUSIC   No. 15c

                        JOSEPHA *crosses below* LEOPOLD *to exit* C. *As she does so, he gives her a playful smack on the behind.*

JOSEPHA [*shocked*]   Leopold!

                        LEOPOLD *laughs.*
                        The lights BLACK-OUT *as—*   LIGHTING CUE 11
                        the RUNNING TABS *close*
                        The music continues.

SCENE 5

Outside the Inn

The scene is now set for the arrival of the Emperor. There is a triumphal arch up C on which is written " WELCOME " There are strings of bunting and a large Austrian flag hangs from the Inn.

When the RUNNING TABS *open,* WORKMEN *are hammering at the arch :* MAIDS *on the balcony* R *are hanging out garlands and streamers. The whole* COMPANY *is there and with various* VILLAGERS *in gala costume are milling about chattering excitedly. Among them are the* FORESTER, *the* MAYOR *and* COUNCILLORS *and* KATHI. KARL *enters from the Inn.* LEOPOLD *enters through the crowd up* R *and meets* KARL C. *The music fades.*

LEOPOLD. Listen, boy. Go round to the gunsmith and tell him to get twenty rounds of ammunition ready to fire a salute, at the end of my speech.

KARL *turns to go.*

[*He restrains him*] I don't want it fired until I've finished my speech, understand? When I say the word " Welcome " you fire.
KARL. I'll fire all right. A blooming bombardment. [*He crosses to* R]
LEOPOLD. Stop!

KARL *stops and turns.*

After what word is it that you fire?
KARL. After " Welcome " of course. I'm not a half-wit.

KARL *exits up* R. LEOPOLD *walks up and down, rehearsing his speech.*

LEOPOLD. " Your Majesty—er . . . Your Majesty—unaccustomed as I am . . . " [*He sees the Mayor*] Ah, your Worship! You're just the man I want. [*He puts the Mayor* RC] Stand over here, will you. Now—you're the Emperor and I'll be me. [*He clears his throat*] " Your Majesty . . . " [*He breaks off*] No, no. Not a bit like it. Stand aside. I can't possibly make a speech to a Corporation. [*He pushes the Mayor aside and turns to the Forester*] Here! You! [*He puts the Forester* RC] You look more like it. " Your Majesty—I take the liberty of wishing you—of wishing you—[*his hand gets entangled with the Forester's beard*] a very merry Christmas." No, no! Go away, Santa Claus, you're cramping my style. [*He pushes the Forester aside*] I know. I've got it! " Your Majesty, on behalf of the whole population I beg to offer you a loyal and hearty welcome."

ALL *applaud.* LEOPOLD *bows right and left.*

FORESTER. " On behalf of the whole population . . . "
MAYOR. " We beg to offer you a loyal and hearty welcome."
LEOPOLD. I must go and change into my official receiver's outfit.

LEOPOLD *exits to the Inn.*
GRINKLE *and* OTTOLINE *enter on the balcony* L.

GRINKLE. Now we shall see what sort of a show these foreigners can put up.
OTTOLINE. But, Daddy . . .
GRINKLE. Don't butt in.

FINALE ACT II

No. 16

LEOPOLD, JOSEPHA, SUTTON *and* CHORUS

A procession of POLICE, TEACHERS, FIREMEN, *etc., enters, led by a* BAND.

ALL. Side by side, with manly pride,
Behold a loyal throng,
Marching along,
Steady and strong.

Bang the drum and blow the trumpet,
Let the bugles blast.
Make way, we pray,
For the Grand March Past.

The band is playing
A loud and lively air,
And to its braying
We stride around the square.
It's rather tiring
But still we don't complain,
For to that martial strain
We all feel young again.
It's so inspiring;
There's pride in ev'ry eye,
And people cheer
Far and near,
When they hear us marching by.

We march along
To the music of the band.
Strong and steady,
With friends on either hand.
And so round and round,
Through the big triumphal arch,
With backs stiff as starch,
Gaily we march.

Hooray!
Here comes the Fire Brigade.
The fiercest flames they love to fight,
Day and night,
Though they're quite unpaid;
Then cheer,
The Fire Brigade is here.
And though they handle water well,
They excel
When they handle beer.

Side by side, with manly pride,
Behold a loyal throng.
Marching along,
Steady and strong,
Bang the drum and blow the trumpet,
Let the bugles blast.
Make way, we pray,
For the Grand March Past.

The band is playing
A loud and lively air,
And to its braying
We stride around the square.
It's rather tiring,
But still we don't complain,
For to that martial strain
We all feel young again.

It's so inspiring;
There's pride in ev'ry eye,
And people cheer,
Far and near,
When they hear us marching by.

GRINKLE. Not a bit of it! They ought to see the Carnival procession at Clacton.

The boat's siren is heard off L.
KARL enters excitedly up R.

KARL. The Emperor—H-h-his Majesty—he's here.

KARL exits up R.

The Steamer appears up L. On it are the EMPEROR, KETTERL, his servant, two AIDES-DE-CAMP, the CAPTAIN and the two SAILORS. While the CHORUS sing the Steamer comes C and is made fast by the SAILORS.

CHORUS.   Hail to His Majesty!
          Long live His Majesty!
          God save His Majesty,
          And bless the Fatherland,
          The Fatherland.

The music continues.

The EMPEROR, KETTERL and the AIDES-DE-CAMP disembark and come down C. The EMPEROR is a dignified and impressive figure, made up to resemble the famous portraits of Franz Joseph as an old man. The populace bow low, and GIRLS strew flowers in his path.

LEOPOLD enters from the Inn. A moment of tense silence ensues. LEOPOLD is almost beside himself with nervous anxiety. He is pushed forward by the MAYOR.

LEOPOLD [*trembling*] Your Majesty ... Oh ... Your Majesty—er—Your Majesty—Your Imperial Majesty—Your Imperial Eagle——

The EMPEROR smiles kindly.

—I mean—give me time, your Majesty—the words are there and they'll come—I'm sure they'll come.

Loud gun-shots are heard off up R.

What's that? [*He frantically waves his hand to stop the firing*] Hey, stop it! I said, "they'll come", not "welcome".

The fusilade increases.

That's done it! I can't think of anything to say, now. I'm stuck. Oh, your Majesty ...
EMPEROR [*kindly*] No need to be nervous, my friend.
LEOPOLD. Good Lord! Wouldn't you be nervous if you had to make a speech to an Emperor? [*He looks around for help*] On behoof—I mean—on behofe ...
ALL [*coming to the rescue*] On behalf of the whole population we beg to offer your Majesty a loyal and hearty welcome.
LEOPOLD. That's it! My very words. That's exactly what I wanted to say.
EMPEROR. I thank you.
LEOPOLD [*airily*] You're welcome. That's nothing at all. I'm no speaker, your Majesty.
EMPEROR. So I noticed.

JOSEPHA and SUTTON enter on the balcony L. SUTTON carries a bouquet of red roses intended for the Emperor.

LEOPOLD. But this is the proudest moment of my life. [*Seriously*] God save your Majesty! God bless our homes! Long live everybody! Hurray!

SCENE 5   WHITE HORSE INN   47

JOSEPHA⎫
SUTTON ⎬ [*together*] Hurray!
      ⎭

                                  SUTTON *hands the bouquet to* JOSEPHA. *She takes it and for a moment allows his hand to rest in hers.*

CHORUS. Hurray!

                                  LEOPOLD *looks up at the balcony* L *in an agony of jealousy.*

LEOPOLD [*in a loud whisper*] Josepha!

                                  JOSEPHA *takes no notice but continues to smile at* SUTTON.

[*He loses control of himself and turns to the* Emperor] One other thing I'd like to tell your Majesty—there's dirty work going on up there.

                                  The CROWD *are horrified and try to stop Leopold.*
                                  JOSEPHA *and* SUTTON *exit from the balcony.*

Take my advice. Don't go near the *White Horse*. She's not to be trusted a yard.

CHORUS [*singing*]   Leopold, oh, Leopold!
                    What are you up to, Leopold?
                    In Heaven's name, then, Leopold,
                    What have you done?

                                  JOSEPHA *and* SUTTON *enter from the Inn. The* MAYOR *and others seize* LEOPOLD *and try to restrain him. He breaks away with a sob.*

LEOPOLD.   I don't care, I vow,
                    All is over, now.
                    What does it matter, anyhow?
                    I've done with women.
                    [*He sobs*]

EMPEROR [*laying his hand on Leopold's*] Come, my friend. Control yourself. You're talking nonsense. Never mind. I'm used to hearing nonsense from my Ministers.

                                  JOSEPHA *sings and offers the roses to the Emperor.*

JOSEPHA [*with a curtsy*]
                    I hope your Majesty will pardon him,
                    And not be hard on him,
                    He's rather scared.
                    If so be, your Majesty, will follow me,
                    I'll show your Majesty the rooms that we've prepared.

EMPEROR [*taking the roses; spoken*] Thank you. [*He turns to Ketterl*] Ketterl. [*He hands the roses to Ketterl and turns to Josepha*] I am delighted to have the opportunity of staying at your well-known Inn. [*He turns to the Crowd*] It is a great pleasure to me to be here among my loyal subjects whose welfare is so very dear to me. [*He salutes*]

                                  The CROWD *form a lane to the Inn door.*

                                  The EMPEROR, *with musical honours, exits to the Inn.* KETTERL *and the* AIDES-DE-CAMP *follow him off.* LEOPOLD *rushes to* JOSEPHA *to try and speak to her. She angrily repulses him, takes a dark red rose from her bodice and pins it on to Sutton's buttonhole.*

                                  JOSEPHA *exits to the Inn. The* CROWD *turn furiously upon Leopold.*

                                  KARL *enters up* R.

CHORUS.   We can't understand
                    Why you're so unmanned,
                    To behave like that.

SUTTON.	Whatever can you have been at?	MUSIC
CHORUS.	Do explain!	
	Were you insane?	
	Explain! Explain!	

LEOPOLD *takes the rose from Sutton's buttonhole and his eyes fill with tears.*

LEOPOLD. It would be wonderful, indeed,
If she could love as I love;
If in her eyes I could but read
Her heart's reply to my love.
CHORUS. She takes the love that he is giving,
And makes his life worth living.
Ah, poor Leopold.
LEOPOLD. She takes the love that I am giving,
And breaks my heart.
[*He breaks down*]
Yes, all my dreams would come true
If I knew
That she loved me, too.

KARL [*spoken*] Pull yourself together. Not in front of the guests.

LEOPOLD. I'll do or die,
You'll know the reason why
When told of bold Leopold's "last stand"
For the Fatherland.
Good-bye. Good-bye.
I wish you all a last Good-bye.
CHORUS. Good-bye. Good-bye. Good-bye.
LEOPOLD *and* CHORUS.
Good-bye. Good-bye.
I wish you all a last Good-bye.

LEOPOLD *exits and* ALL *wave a farewell as—*

the CURTAIN *falls*

ACT III

SCENE 1

Outside the Inn

Down L, *an elegant table with a lace cloth and flowers is laid for breakfast.*

ENTR'ACTE AND SERENADE   No. 17

CHORUS

When the CURTAIN *rises, it is early in the morning of the following day. The Village Choral Society, in gala costume, has met beneath the Emperor's window to serenade him. The* MAYOR, KARL *and others are also present.* SIGISMUND *conducts the choir, which sings with comic variation in volume of voices as indicated in the vocal score.*

CHORUS.   Softly!   Softly!
          Softly!   Softly!
          Hark the village choir parading
          Softly!   Softly!
          Start their loyal serenading
          Hark!   With voices low and gentle,
          Sing we something sentimental.
          Softly!   Softly!
          Choosing a reposeful number
          That shall not disturb his slumber.

                         KARL *carries on singing after the others have stopped and is chased into the Inn by* SIGISMUND.

                         The EMPEROR *enters on the balcony* L. *He wears his shooting costume.*

EMPEROR.   My friends, I thank you most sincerely for a very unique performance. I can truthfully say that I have seldom heard anything at all like it.

                         The EMPEROR *exits from the balcony.*

SIGISMUND.   His Majesty will be down in a minute, and then, remember, a good hearty cheer.
MAN.   Here he comes.
SIGISMUND.   Hip!   Hip! ...
ALL.   Hurrah!

                         GRINKLE *enters from the Inn.*

GRINKLE.   Thank you. All this is very flattering, I'm sure. They certainly never dreamt of welcoming me like this at Clacton. [*To Sigismund*] Your idea? And you're a conductor, too, I see.
SIGISMUND.   Yes. I can conduct anything. From a bus to a successful love-affair.
GRINKLE.   Aha! I've heard all about that. [*He whispers*] How's it getting on, eh?
SIGISMUND.   I didn't know you knew.
GRINKLE [*digging him in the ribs*] I'm much cleverer than you think.
SIGISMUND.   That's more than probable. But I didn't know you knew about me and—her.
GRINKLE.   A charming girl, though I say it as shouldn't.
SIGISMUND.   Why shouldn't you?
GRINKLE.   Why not, indeed? [*Archly*] You rogue, eh?
SIGISMUND.   Of course, the Emperor being here is a bit of luck for me. I may persuade him to give

our firm a Royal Warrant. " By appointment to His Imperial Majesty ", eh ? But I understand the old gentleman's not very easy to tackle. A bit peppery, I believe, eh, what ?

The EMPEROR *enters from the Inn.* KETTERL *follows him on. The* CROWD *bow very low, with their heads nearly touching the ground.* GRINKLE *nudges* SIGISMUND *who sees the Emperor and waves to the* CROWD *to cheer, but they remain silently bowed.*

Too late ! [*To Grinkle*] That's what comes of your talking so much.
MAYOR [*to the Emperor*] Your Majesty, may I have the honour of presenting Herr Sigismund Smith, son of the well-known English woollen manufacturer.
SIGISMUND. We specialize in underwear, your Majesty.
EMPEROR. Very interesting, I'm sure.
SIGISMUND. Yes. As I was saying to my father only the other day—we were speaking of your Majesty —we very often speak of your Majesty in my family . . .

GRINKLE, *wishing to be presented, nudges Sigismund.*

EMPEROR [*smiling*] Very kind of you.
SIGISMUND. Yes. As I was saying only a week ago . . .

GRINKLE *nudges Sigismund.*

[*To Grinkle*] What's the matter ? Oh, yes. This is Mr Grinkle, your Majesty. He is also in woollen underwear.
GRINKLE [*pushing Sigismund aside*] Made only of best quality wool that always comes up to scratch. [*He beams with joviality*] Delighted to meet you. [*He holds out his hand*]

The EMPEROR *hesitates a moment, then shakes hands with Grinkle.*

Hope you're fit and flourishing, eh ?
EMPEROR. I am very well, thank you. You are a stranger here, I think ?
GRINKLE. Yes. Like you ; just on a visit, you know. I'd sooner have gone to Clacton, as we usually do, but my daughter—well, you know what girls are. [*He winks and nudges the Emperor*]
EMPEROR. Quite so ! Quite so ! [*He turns to Sigismund*] You were telling me about your business. I have always wondered where you people get your raw material.
GRINKLE [*aside*] So have I. [*He listens jealously for Sigismund's reply*]
SIGISMUND. Certainly, your Majesty—I shall be delighted to tell you. [*He whispers in the Emperor's ear*]
GRINKLE [*aside*] Very rude to whisper in public.
EMPEROR [*to Sigismund*] Indeed ?
SIGISMUND. It's a trade secret, your Majesty. You won't give me away ?
EMPEROR. I can assure you, my friend, I am the soul of discretion.
SIGISMUND. Yes. I'd always heard that.

A hard-faced, steel-spectacled female, who is President of the Girls' Friendly Society, interposes herself, between Sigismund and the Emperor.

LADY PRESIDENT [*twittering*] If you please, your Majesty. [*She bows so low that her face is invisible*]
EMPEROR. What is this ?
MAYOR. Just a formality, your Majesty. May I present the Lady President of the Young Girls' Friendly Society, that's all. Not very young herself, but extremely friendly.
EMPEROR. If the lady might perhaps let me see her face . . .

The LADY PRESIDENT *straightens up and beams at the Emperor.*

[*He gives her a look*] No. Never mind. [*He motions to her to bow again*]

The LADY PRESIDENT *bows and retires.*

JOSEPHA *enters from the Inn.* Two WAITRESSES *follow her on. They carry breakfast dishes which they put on the table* L.

JOSEPHA [*with a curtsy*] Breakfast, your Majesty.

The two WAITRESSES *exit to the Inn.*

SCENE 1   WHITE HORSE INN

SIGISMUND. We will not trespass any longer on your Majesty's time. [*He signs to the Crowd*]   **MUSIC**

The CROWD *curtsy and bow to the Emperor and exit. The* EMPEROR *waves kindly at them.*

SIGISMUND *and* GRINKLE *exit to the Inn.* JOSEPHA *and the* EMPEROR *are left alone.*

JOSEPHA. Breakfast's ready, your Majesty. Would your Majesty like to sit here—in the sun?

The EMPEROR *moves to the table* L *and sits.*

Shall I butter a roll for you?
EMPEROR. Thank you.

JOSEPHA *butters a roll.*

Not too much butter. I'm slimming.
JOSEPHA. You don't need to—I beg your pardon, your Majesty—I mean . . .
EMPEROR [*smiling*] That's all right.
JOSEPHA. I want to say, too, how sorry I am about yesterday.
EMPEROR. Yesterday?
JOSEPHA. The head waiter's behaviour. I hope you've forgiven it.
EMPEROR. Oh, that? [*He laughs*]
JOSEPHA. You see, your Majesty, he's not been quite himself lately. A little bit upset. In fact—he's gone rather queer in the head, I think.
EMPEROR. And in the heart, too, perhaps? [*He looks at her*] Well, it's quite understandable.
JOSEPHA. It's not really *my* fault, your Majesty—not altogether, at least . . .
EMPEROR. I'm sure it isn't.
JOSEPHA. Life's rather difficult—for a widow.
EMPEROR [*smiling*] And for a widower.
JOSEPHA. Yes, your Majesty. You see . . . [*She breaks off*]
EMPEROR. Go on, my dear. Tell me about it.
JOSEPHA. Well—it's like this. There's a lawyer from London—very grand, you know, and smart—and he's been rather attentive—and—somehow—I thought—I thought perhaps he might—that I might—that we might—but then I'm not sure if he's quite—or—if—I—you see . . .
EMPEROR [*smiling*] It all sounds rather complicated.
JOSEPHA. Yes, your Majesty, it is. But I don't know why I should worry you with my private affairs—you who have so many more important things to worry about.
EMPEROR. Yes. Life isn't always easy, is it? But so long as one does one's best—eh? [*He taps her hand kindly*] Ah, my dear child—when I was your age I, too, used often to wonder what I should make of life—what I should become. [*He sighs*] And what have I made of it—what have I become?
JOSEPHA. An Emperor, your Majesty.
EMPEROR [*sadly*] An Emperor. Yes.
JOSEPHA. It must be marvellous.
EMPEROR. I wonder.
JOSEPHA. Oh—and, your Majesty—do you think I could ask you a very great favour?
EMPEROR. I'm sure you could.
JOSEPHA. It's only this—could you—would you write in my book? [*She takes a small book and a fountain pen from her pocket*]
EMPEROR. Your book?
JOSEPHA. My birthday book. [*She hands the book and pen to the Emperor*] If you'd just write something—something I could always look at—something that would help me—when things are a little—difficult.
EMPEROR. I'll do my best.

RECITATION

EMPEROR

The EMPEROR *ponders a moment then writes in the book.*

EMPEROR. "In this fickle world today,
All things change and pass away;
Even love, they say,
May grow cold.
Happiness is hard to find,
Yet shall Fate, too long unkind,
Bring you peace of mind,
When you're old.

Prudence, all in vain, may preach
That which Time alone can teach;
Though the joys of which we dream
Always seem
Out of reach.

Failing love and happiness,
Be content with something less.
Wait, and face the world meanwhile
With a smile.

The EMPEROR *closes the book and returns it to* JOSEPHA, *who kisses his hand. The sound of hunting horns is heard off.*

The FORESTER *and two* GAMEKEEPERS *enter up* R.

KETTERL *enters from the Inn. He carries a shot-gun.*

FORESTER. Your Majesty. Everything is ready.
EMPEROR [*rising; with a laugh*] Good gracious me! I'd forgotten all about the shoot.

KETTERL *hands the gun to the* EMPEROR *who puts it under his left arm.*

[*To Josepha*] Thank you again for your hospitality. I enjoyed our little talk—[*he smiles*] and I'm sure you're very discreet.

JOSEPHA *curtsies. The* EMPEROR *crosses to the exit down* R.

KARL *enters from the Inn in a great hurry. He carries a bill.*

KARL [*rushing to the Emperor*] Your Majesty. The bill. You haven't paid the bill.
JOSEPHA. Karl! [*To the Emperor*] I'm sorry, your Majesty. It's just a silly mistake. [*To Karl*] I'm ashamed of you.
KARL. I'm sorry, your Majesty. Good luck, your Majesty. And good sport. [*He holds out his hand*] I hope everything was quite satisfactory.

The EMPEROR *feels in his pocket and gives Karl a coin.*

EMPEROR. You young rascal!

The EMPEROR *taps Karl on the cheek, turns and exits down* R.
The FORESTER, KETTERL *and the* GAMEKEEPERS *follow him off.*
KARL *stands stiffly at the salute until they have gone.*

KARL [*looking at the coin*] Well, I'm blowed! It's high time we had a republic.
JOSEPHA. Don't you dare speak like that. Oh—I know who's been putting those ideas into your silly head. Leopold, eh? Get out before I lose my temper. [*She threatens Karl*]

KARL *runs up* R.
LEOPOLD *enters* R *and collides with Karl, who exits up* R.

[*She turns to Leopold*] It's you, is it? What do you want?
LEOPOLD. Nothing. I merely came to say good-bye, that's all.
JOSEPHA. Again?
LEOPOLD. There are some things one can't say too often.
JOSEPHA. There's one thing I'm waiting for you to say.
LEOPOLD. What's that?
JOSEPHA. That you're sorry for your behaviour yesterday.
LEOPOLD. The only thing I'm sorry for about yesterday *is* that I should have thought you were a friend of mine, that I could trust you. It was a mistake. It shan't occur again. Well—good-bye, then. And this time, mind you, I shall *not* come back. [*He turns to exit down* R]
JOSEPHA. I wonder.
LEOPOLD [*stopping and turning*] What do you mean—" you wonder "?
JOSEPHA. Oh, nothing, nothing. Don't let me keep you.
LEOPOLD [*hesitating*] No, I won't. I've got to go down to the Mayor's office to see about a passport.
JOSEPHA. You're leaving the country?
LEOPOLD. Everything I had planned and hoped for has been shattered. So I shall seek fresh fields overseas.

LEOPOLD *exits down* R.

JOSEPHA [*calling after him*] Leopold? [*She turns away*] Oh, well! Perhaps it's all for the best.

SUTTON *enters from the Inn*.

[*She moves down* C] Ah? You!
SUTTON [*moving to* L *of Josepha*] Yes. Me. Anything wrong? You look sad.
JOSEPHA. No. [*She tries to brighten up*] Nothing wrong. I'm very happy, really.
SUTTON. Was the Emperor satisfied?
JOSEPHA. Quite. And you? Are you satisfied, too?
SUTTON. Who wouldn't be—here?

The RUNNING TABS *close behind Sutton and Josepha*

REPRISE No. 18a

SUTTON, OTTOLINE *and* JOSEPHA

SUTTON.   The *White Horse Inn!*
          At the *White Horse Inn*,
          There's joy the whole summer through.

OTTOLINE *enters* R. SUTTON *moves quickly to her*

OTTOLINE *and* SUTTON.   There's sunshine ever in store there,
                         And happiness stands at the door there.

OTTOLINE *gives* SUTTON *a little sign. He takes Josepha's hand and kisses it as though in farewell*

SUTTON.   The days fly past,
          You must leave at last.

OTTOLINE *and* SUTTON *move* R.

OTTOLINE *and* SUTTON.   But still, whatever you do,
                         You'll hear, when twilight is falling,
                         The *White Horse* calling to you.

OTTOLINE *and* SUTTON *exit* R. JOSEPHA *looks sadly after them grasps the situation, takes her book from her pocket and reads.*

JOSEPHA. In this fickle world today,
All things change and pass away;
Even love, they say,
May grow cold.

Happiness is hard to find,
Yet shall Fate, too long unkind,
Bring you peace of mind,
When you're old.
[*She moves* L]

Prudence, all in vain, may preach
That which Time alone can teach;
Though the joys of which we dream
Always seem
Out of reach.

Failing love and happiness,
Be content with something less.
Wait, and face the world meanwhile
With a smile.

JOSEPHA *exits sadly* L *as—*

the lights BLACK-OUT

LIGHTING CUE 12

SCENE 2

"*The Travellers' Rest*"

The drop-cloth depicts the exterior of the building with a view of the pine forest and mountains. A house-piece R *has doors into the building. Rustic tables and chairs are set* RC *and* LC.

When the RUNNING TABS *open a party of* GUIDES *and* CLIMBERS, *equipped with ropes, knapsacks, alpenstocks, etc., are being served with beer in "steins" by the* LANDLORD.

TYROLEAN DANCE   No. 18b

MALE DANCERS *and* CHORUS

After the Dance, to which the GUIDES *and* CLIMBERS *clap to time and generally "whoop" and make merry, the* DANCERS *and* CHORUS *exit* R *and* L. *The* LANDLORD *exits* R.

GRINKLE *enters* L. *He wears his Tyrolean outfit. He turns and beckons off* L.

GRINKLE [*calling*] Come on, lightning.

HINZEL *enters* L. *He is on the point of exhaustion. He sits* L *of the table* LC. GRINKLE *sits* R *of the table* LC.

The LANDLORD *enters* R *and crosses to* LC. *He carries a tray with two "steins" of beer.* GRINKLE *snatches one of the steins and "downs" the beer in one. The* LANDLORD *and* HINZEL *watch spellbound. The* LANDLORD *offers the second stein to Hinzel.*

[*He takes the second stein*] No, no. I think he'd prefer oxygen. [*He downs the beer in one*]

SUTTON *and* OTTOLINE *enter* R.

OTTOLINE [*crossing to* LC] Hello, Daddy. Having a nice climb?

GRINKLE [*crossly*] I'm beginning to feel like a mountain goat. [*He rises*] Get the Professor to show you the view, my dear, but don't let him rush you. I've got something to say to our friend here. [*He crosses to Sutton*]

OTTOLINE *sits* R *of the table* LC *and talks with* HINZEL.

[*To Sutton*] How are things going?
SUTTON. Splendidly! I've had a wire from old Smith today—he's delighted to hear of his son's engagement.
GRINKLE. Good. But—does Ottoline know she's engaged?
SUTTON. Give me time. I'm breaking it to her gradually. By tonight everything should be settled.
GRINKLE. I hope so. I've ordered a magnificent supper—to celebrate the engagement. No expense spared. Hock-cup flowing like water—and probably tasting like it, too, I expect—and any number of cress sandwiches. A swell affair, I tell you. [*He turns to Ottoline*] See you later, Ottie. Take my advice and go into consultation with the well-known firm of Sutton, Sutton, Sutton and Sutton, and you may hear of something to your advantage, eh? Ha! Ha! [*To Hinzel*] Come along, Professor. It'll be *downhill* this time.

HINZEL *rises and exits with* GRINKLE R.

"MY SONG OF LOVE" No. 19

OTTOLINE, SUTTON, CHORUS *and* DANCERS

OTTOLINE *rises and moves to Sutton.*

OTTOLINE [*speaking over the music*] You're a very bad man, I'm afraid.
SUTTON [*laughing*] Shall we climb a little further?
OTTOLINE. No. Let's talk.
SUTTON. What about?
OTTOLINE. Ourselves.

SUTTON [*singing*]   There's no need to tell you, dear,
What I feel.
I have nothing now to fear
Or conceal.
Yet no falt'ring words of mine
Can define
How I pine
For a sign that you're mine.

OTTOLINE.   Music, so they say, has charms,
And perchance,
When you hold me in your arms
As we dance
Love shall whisper soft and low
To hearts aglow.
SUTTON.   That is so.
For I know.

My song of love is a waltz refrain.
'Tis heard above ev'ry other strain.
With an art sublime
Ev'ry phrase is built,
And my heart beats time
To the rhyme and the lilt.

BOTH.	My senses thrill to that music sweet, And faster still do my pulses beat, All around, where its echoes resound, " Love is kind ", it seems to say, " Come and find it while you may ". All life through, where such music is found Love can make the world go waltzing round. *The* CHORUS *enter* R *and* L.
OTTOLINE.	There's no song a lover sings On this earth Like the tune that always brings Love to birth. There's no music half so fair Anywhere I declare None shall dare to compare.
SUTTON.	When I hear each magic note, Night or day, On the air I seem to float Far away. And I feel that I possess true happiness. Then, ah, yes, I confess :
ALL.	My song of love is a waltz refrain. 'Tis heard above ev'ry other strain. With an art sublime Ev'ry phrase is built, And my heart beats time, To the rhyme and the lilt.
BOTH.	My senses thrill to that music sweet, And faster still do my pulses beat, All around, where its echoes resound, " Love is kind ", it seems to say, " Come and find it while you may ". All life through, where such music is found Love can make the world go waltzing round. *The* DANCERS *enter and dance as the* CHORUS *sing*.
ENSEMBLE.	My senses thrill to that music sweet, And faster still do my pulses beat, All around, where its echoes resound, " Love is kind ", it seems to say, " Come and find it while you may ". All life through, where such music is found, Love can make the world go waltzing round My song of love is a waltz refrain, Waltz refrain, Waltz refrain. Song of love.

The number ends with a picture.

EXIT MUSIC

All exit R and L.
SIGISMUND *and* GRETEL *enter* R. *The music fades.*

MUSIC
No. 19a

SIGISMUND. Well, here we are. Two thousand feet above the level of the sea. On the top of the world. And I'm on the top of my form, too. Let's sit down and look at the view—or, rather, *you* look at the view and I'll look at you.

GRETEL *sits* L *of the table* RC.

[*He sits* R *of the table* RC] Happy?
GRETEL. Very happy.
SIGISMUND. It's sad to think that I should ever have to go back to Hammersmith. Couldn't you come with me?
GRETEL. No. I couldn't.
SIGISMUND. Why not? Anything the matter with Hammersmith?
GRETEL. Ye*th*. It-*th* got an *eth* in it.
SIGISMUND. If only you'd let me give you a few lessons in elocution you wouldn't worry over a little thing like that.
GRETEL. Do you really think *tho*?
SIGISMUND. I know it. Won't you let me try? I'll start a night-school with you as my only pupil. We'd begin with a simple lesson, on some easy word. Now, let me think, what's an easy word? Well, let's take " love ".
GRETEL [*timidly*] Oh, no!
SIGISMUND. Lesson one : conjugate the verb " To love ". " I love, thou loves*, he loves . . . " Try.
GRETEL. " I love, thou love*th*t . . . " No, I can't.
SIGISMUND. You're going too fast. " I love."
GRETEL. " I love."
SIGISMUND. " I love, thou . . . "
GRETEL. " I love, thou . . . "
SIGISMUND. No. That's not grammar. You must say " I love *you* ".
GRETEL. " I love *you*." Oh. [*She rises and moves down* C]
SIGISMUND [*rising and moving to* R *of her*] And I love *you*.

GRETEL *and* SIGISMUND *fall into each other's arms.*
The RUNNING TABS *close behind Gretel and Sigismund*

Gretel !
GRETEL. Thigi*th*mund !

REPRISE

GRETEL *and* SIGISMUND

No. 19b

GRETEL.	Oh, Sigismund, you've simply stunned me with your beauty.
	I never met a greater pet in all my life.
SIGISMUND.	You're lovely, too, and we should do a public duty,
	And help mankind if we combined as man and wife.
GRETEL.	You're just the man a woman *can* be satisfied with.
SIGISMUND.	And you're a gal I always shall be mad about.
BOTH.	There may be thousands whom, I vow, I could reside with,
	But you're the only one I couldn't live without,
	But you're the only one I couldn't do without.

GRETEL *and* SIGISMUND *dance off* L *as—*
the lights BLACK-OUT

LIGHTING CUE 13

The music continues.

Scene 3

Outside the Inn

A string of lanterns stretches between the buildings R *and* L. *There is a small table and chair down* L.
When the RUNNING TABS *open, lights are twinkling in the distant houses across the lake and gleam from the doorways and windows of the " White Horse Inn ". The hanging lanterns are lit. To soft music,* JOSEPHA *enters from the Inn. She carries two triple candlesticks which she places on the table down* L. LEOPOLD *enters down* R. *He is wearing a light overcoat and carries a suitcase and a bird-cage.*

JOSEPHA. Back again, I see.

The music fades.

LEOPOLD. Only for a moment. I've packed my trunk and watered the canary, given the dog his " din-din " and now I'm off for good. There's only one thing I nearly forgot. [*He puts the bag and cage on the ground*]

JOSEPHA. Only one thing?

LEOPOLD. I want a reference. [*He hands her a notebook*]

JOSEPHA. You want a character? From *me?*

LEOPOLD. Yes. Just sit down, will you, and write me a letter of recommendation. That's all I want.

JOSEPHA [*moving* L] That's all. [*She sits at the table*] You may not like it very much when it's written.

LEOPOLD. Possibly not. I'll risk it. Here! [*He takes a pen and an inkpot from his pocket and puts them on the table*] Now, go ahead.

JOSEPHA. But I don't know what to write.

LEOPOLD. I'll tell you : " The bearer of this——

JOSEPHA *writes.*

was in my service as head waiter for six months . . . "

JOSEPHA. But it was only six weeks.

LEOPOLD. I know. But six months sounds better. Anyhow, it felt like six years. Go on : " I always found him honest, hard-working, respectable, and frequently sober—— "

JOSEPHA. Now, *Leopold!*

LEOPOLD. " —clean in his habits and person and ' house-trained '." Have you got that? You might add : " good-tempered and industrious ".

JOSEPHA [*writing*] How do you spell " industrious "?

LEOPOLD. I don't know. The usual way, I suppose, with a couple of us's. Don't interrupt. " He left of his own free will."

JOSEPHA. " To better himself ", I suppose?

LEOPOLD. No. [*He is carried away by his feelings*] " He left because he couldn't bear it any longer. Because he couldn't stand by and see the only woman he ever loved being made a fool of by another man. He couldn't stay and see his dreams shattered—his hopes wrecked. He left of his own accord —and with a broken heart." [*He turns away*] Have you got that?

JOSEPHA. Yes, I've got that. [*She rises and hands the book to him*]

LEOPOLD. Thank you. [*He takes a roll-blotter from his pocket and blots the writing*] Well. That's all, then. Good-bye. [*He picks up his bag and cage*]

JOSEPHA. Good-bye, Leopold. Good luck and—[*tenderly*] God bless you.

LEOPOLD. And God bless you. [*He moves slowly up* R *then stops and turns*] Did you say anything?

JOSEPHA. No.

LEOPOLD. You didn't call or anything?

JOSEPHA. No.

LEOPOLD. You're not angry with me?

JOSEPHA [*moving* C] Angry? Yes, Leopold, I am. Very angry. I'm furious to find how little you know me, how little you understand me.

LEOPOLD. But . . . [*He drops his bag and cage and moves to* R *of her*]

JOSEPHA. Don't say another word. You haven't read what I've written yet.

LEOPOLD. But . . .

JOSEPHA. Go on. Read it.

LEOPOLD [*almost sobbing*] Of course, if you want me to. [*He reads the book*] It's very difficult to read —[*he wipes a tear from his eye*] it's rather blurred and there are several blots. [*He looks closely at the writing*] What? [*He reads*] "... obstinate ... jealous ... masterful ... discharged as head waiter for interfering in his employer's private affairs ..." That's not true. "... subsequently re-engaged ..."? What do you mean by "re-engaged"?
JOSEPHA. Read on.
LEOPOLD [*reading*] "... re-engaged for life as Manager and Part Proprietor of the *White Horse Inn*." Part Proprietor! For life! You mean "till death do us part"? Josepha!
JOSEPHA [*with feeling*] Leopold!
LEOPOLD. Josepha, do you really mean it?
JOSEPHA. If you'll take on the job?
LEOPOLD. Take it on! Oh, Josepha! [*He throws his hat in the air and embraces her*]
JOSEPHA. You're disarranging my hair.
LEOPOLD [*excitedly*] Your hair! Good Heavens! I'll disarrange a lot more before I've done. Whoop! I'll show them how to run a hotel. [*He tears off his overcoat, throws it off R and pulls the tails of his evening coat out of his pockets*] Old Grinkle's giving a big party tonight, isn't he? Well, it's going to be the biggest ever seen if I have anything to do with it. [*He calls*] Waiter. Karl. Boy.

KARL, *holding up a metal tray, enters from the Inn.*

KARL. All right! All right! I'm coming! A waiter's a human being, isn't he?
LEOPOLD [*knocking the tray out of Karl's hand*] Not in my hotel. How dare you?
KARL. But you always said ...
LEOPOLD. When I was a waiter, yes—but now I'm proprietor everything's different.
KARL. Proprietor?
LEOPOLD. Yes. *I* am the *White Horse*, I am. Ha! Ha! And ...

KARL *picks up the tray and runs into the Inn.*

JOSEPHA. Do control yourself, Leopold.
LEOPOLD. Not tonight, Josepha. Later on, perhaps. In twenty-five years' time when we celebrate our silver wedding, then, if I come to you again for a character ...
JOSEPHA. I hope I shall be able to say that you were "honest, hard-working, sober, industrious ..."
LEOPOLD. But masterful, eh? Still masterful. Aha! And in years to come when our children's children tell the story ...
JOSEPHA. Aren't you being a bit premature, Leopold?

LEOPOLD *seizes* JOSEPHA *in a warm embrace, which is held, oblivious to everything.*
GRINKLE *and* HINZEL *enter down* R.

GRINKLE. What on earth is happening? Is he murdering the woman?
HINZEL. I don't think so. They seem to be great friends.
GRINKLE. Yes. Now I come to look at them, I think they must have met before. [*He moves to Leopold and taps him on the shoulder*]

LEOPOLD *does not respond.*

Excuse me.

LEOPOLD *does not respond.*

[*To Hinzel*] Saloon's not open—let's try the four-ale bar. [*He moves behind Josepha and taps her on the back*]

JOSEPHA *tears herself away from Leopold and with a cry of joy and dismay runs into the Inn.*

[*To Leopold*] Pardon me, I don't want to interrupt what appears to be a very agreeable round game, but you haven't forgotten, I hope, that I've got a big party on tonight?
LEOPOLD. That's quite all right. A betrothal party, I understand. For Josepha and me.
GRINKLE. Not at all.
LEOPOLD. Who for, then? I don't see any other happy pairs about. Where are they?

                              SUTTON *enters from the Inn.*

SUTTON [*to Hinzel*] Here! Professor, let me present the newly engaged couple.
                         GRETEL *and* SIGISMUND *enter from the Inn.*
                         LEOPOLD *exits to the Inn.*

HINZEL [*astonished*] But—my children . . .
SIGISMUND [*falling on Hinzel's neck*] Papa!
GRINKLE. Here! Hi! What's the meaning of this? [*To Sutton*] Didn't you promise to get my daughter Ottoline engaged?
SUTTON. Quite right. And so I have. [*He calls*] Ottoline.
                         OTTOLINE *enters from the Inn.*
[*To Ottoline*] You're engaged, aren't you?
OTTOLINE. Of course I am.
GRINKLE. And who to, may I ask?
OTTOLINE. You needn't ask. [*She throws herself into Sutton's arms*]
GRINKLE. I forbid the banns.
SUTTON [*falling on Grinkle's neck*] Father!
GRINKLE. This could never have happened at Clacton. What's the next surprise, I wonder?

                         LEOPOLD, JOSEPHA *and two* WAITERS *enter from the Inn. The* WAITERS *carry trays with filled glasses of champagne.* LEOPOLD, JOSEPHA, OTTOLINE, SUTTON, GRETEL, SIGISMUND, GRINKLE *and* HINZEL *each take a glass of champagne.*

LEOPOLD. Champagne! To drink the health of the three happy couples.
GRINKLE. Champagne? But I distinctly ordered hock-cup, and I prefer hock.
LEOPOLD. Nonsense! Champagne's the only wine on such occasions.
GRINKLE. Which do you prefer, my friends?
PRINCIPALS [*in unison*] It's all the same to us.

                              FINALE ACT III   No. 20

                                   ENSEMBLE
                    The CHORUS *and* DANCERS, *in Finale costume, enter waltzing.*

SUTTON.	My song of love is a waltz refrain
OTTOLINE.	'Tis heard above ev'ry other strain.
LEOPOLD.	With an art sublime
	Ev'ry phrase is built,
JOSEPHA.	And my heart beats time
	To the rhyme and the lilt.
SIGISMUND.	My senses thrill to that music sweet
GRETEL.	And faster still do my pulses beat.
ALL.	All around, where its echoes resound,
	" Love is kind ", it seems to say,
	" Come and find it while you may ".
	All life through where such music is found
	Love can make the world go waltzing round.

JOSEPHA *and* LEOPOLD.
                    In Salzkammergut, Salzkammergut,
                    Come what may,
                    Life's as bright and gay as can be.

There's joy to be found
All Summer round,
Night and day,
That's the time for play, you'll agree.

ALL.
There's happiness there;
You can banish trouble and care,
Finding fun and laughter where'er you may go.
For there in the Spring young lovers bring
Songs to sing,
And you hear them yodelling,
" Holdrio ".

the CURTAIN *falls*

FINALE ULTIMO

ENSEMBLE

ALL.
The *White Horse Inn,* at the *White Horse Inn,*
There's joy the whole summer through.
There's sunshine ever in store there,
Your happiness stands at the door there.
The days fly past,
You must leave at last,
But still, whatever you do,
You'll hear, when twilight is falling,
The *White Horse* calling to you.
The *White Horse Inn.*

FINAL CURTAIN

FURNITURE AND PROPERTY LIST

ACT I
SCENE 1

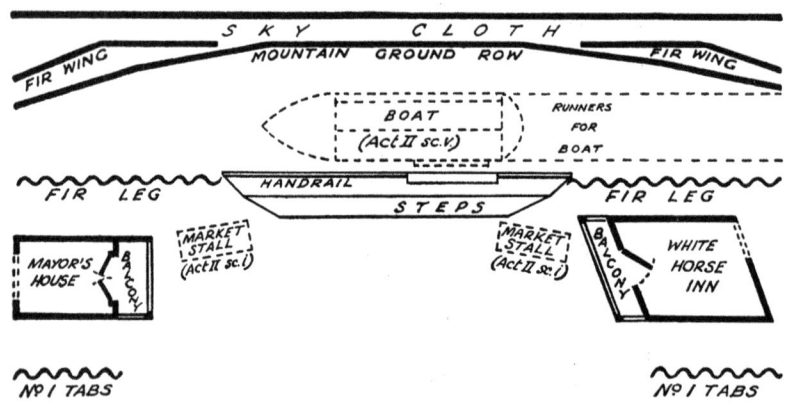

On stage—Gaily painted tubs with small trees
    2 small tables
    3 chairs
    Inn sign
Off stage— Rug (MAIDSERVANT)
    Duster (MAIDSERVANT)
    Wheelbarrow. *In it;* potted flowers (1ST MAN)
    Baskets. *In them;* fruit, vegetables, lobsters, other colourful provisions (2ND MAN)
    Leather post pouch. *In it;* bundle of letters (KATHI)
    2 check tablecloths (KARL)
    Gun (FORESTER)
    Megaphone (COURIER)
    Long trestle table. *On it;* white cloth, plates, cups and saucers, rolls, butter, fruit, etc. (WAITERS)
    2 benches (WAITERS)
    Pots of coffee WAITRESSES)

Jugs of milk (WAITRESSES)
Bill pad, pencil (LEOPOLD)
Coins (TOURISTS)
Alpenstocks, haversacks (ALPINE GUIDES)
Baskets of flowers (FLOWER SELLERS)
Luggage (TRAVELLERS)
2 bags (GRINKLE)
Light case (OTTOLINE)
Napkin (LEOPOLD)
Telegram (LEOPOLD)
Covered dish (KARL)
Suitcase (SUTTON)
Posy of white roses (GRINKLE)

Personal—JOSEPHA : roses
    OTTOLINE : handbag. *In it;* pocket dictionary
    GRINKLE : straw hat. *In band;* 2 steamer tickets, handkerchief
    LEOPOLD : hotel forms, fountain pen
    SUTTON : telegram

SCENE 2

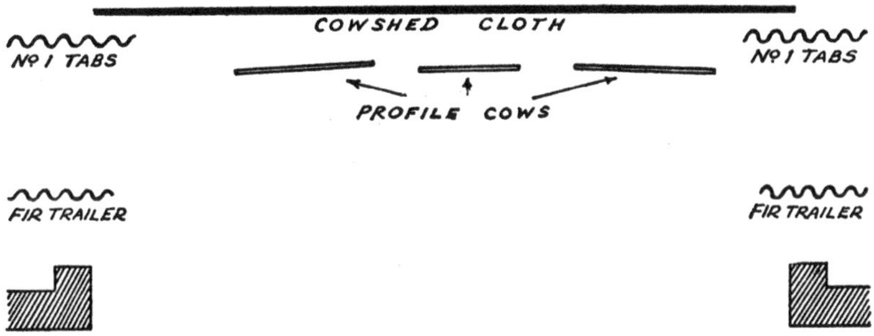

On stage—3 profile cows
3 stools

Setting as Scene 1
Off stage—Umbrellas (GUESTS)

SCENE 3

ACT II
SCENE 1

Main setting as previous scene
Strike—Tables and chairs
Set—Market stall (up RC). *On it;* chickens, sausages, bacon, sucking-pigs
Market stall (up LC). *On it;* vegetables, peaches, apricots, cherries
Off stage—Basket. *In it;* daffodils (MARKET-WOMAN)
Basket. *In it;* edelweiss (MARKET-WOMAN)
Tray. *On it;* heart-shaped gingerbread (MARKET-WOMAN)

Tray. *On it;* pipes, including a meerschaum (MARKET-WOMAN)
Tray. *On it;* chocolates (MARKET-WOMAN)
Shopping basket (LEOPOLD)
Visiting card (KARL)
Small bag. *In it;* candle (HINZEL)
Registered letter (KATHI)

Personal—LEOPOLD : cigarette in long holder
HINZEL : money

SCENE 2

On stage—Rustic bench

SCENE 3

On stage—Long table. *On it;* bell, papers
Chairs as required

Scene 4

On stage—nil

Setting as Act I, Scene 1
On stage—Triumphal arch " WELCOME "
    Bunting
    Austrian flag

Scene 5

Off stage—Flowers (CHORUS GIRLS)
    Bouquet of red roses (SUTTON)
Personal—JOSEPHA: rose

ACT III
Scene 1

Setting as previous scene
On stage—Table. On it; lace cloth, vase of flowers, breakfast things for one, rolls, butter
    Chair

Off stage—2 covered silver dishes (WAITRESSES)
    Shot-gun (KETTERL)
    Bill (KARL)
Personal—JOSEPHA: birthday book, fountain pen
    EMPEROR: coin

Scene 2

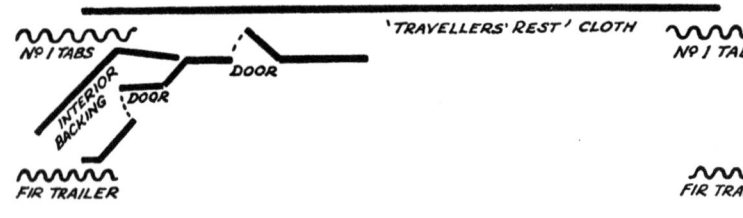

On stage—2 rustic tables
    4 rustic chairs
    " Steins " as required

Off stage—Climbing ropes (CHORUS)
    Alpenstocks (CHORUS)
    Haversacks (CHORUS)
    Tray. On it; 2 steins of beer (LANDLORD)

Scene 3

Setting as Act I, Scene 1
Strike—Arch, bunting and flag
On stage—Table (down L). On it; cloth
    Chair (down L)
Off stage—2 triple candlesticks, lit (JOSEPHA)
    Suitcase (LEOPOLD)

Bird-cage (LEOPOLD)
Metal tray (KARL)
2 trays. On them; 8 glasses of champagne
    (WAITERS)
Personal—LEOPOLD: notebook, inkpot, pen, roll-blotter

LIGHTING PLOT

Property Fittings Required: hanging lanterns, 2 triple candlesticks (all practical)

ACT I SCENE 1 Exterior
To open; Dawn effect, the light pale and shimmering
Cue 1 After rise of CURTAIN (page 1)
   Bring lights slowly up to full sunlight effect

ACT I SCENE 2 Exterior
To open; Effect of sunlight
No cues

ACT I SCENE 3 Exterior
To open; the whole stage flooded with blue light
Cue 2 LEOPOLD [*singing*] "The cows are (page 21)
   blue and so are you"
   Change lights to sunlight effect
Cue 3 GUESTS [*singing*] "The White Horse (page 22)
   Inn . . ."
   Dim lights for "storm" effect
Cue 4 LEOPOLD [*singing*] "On this lovely (page 23)
   summer's day . . ."
   Flash of lightning
Cue 5 LEOPOLD [*singing*] "That gave me (page 23)
   quite a fright"
   Flash of lightning
Cue 6 GUESTS [*singing*] "For lightning and (page 23)
   for thunder . . ."
   Intermittent flashes of lightning until the CURTAIN
   falls

ACT II SCENE 1 Exterior
To open; Effect of sunlight
Cue 7 At end of Scene (page 38)
   Dim to BLACK-OUT

ACT II SCENE 2 Exterior **frontcloth**
To open; Effect of daylight

Cue 8 At end of Scene (page 40)
   Dim to BLACK-OUT

ACT II SCENE 3 Interior
To open; Effect of daylight
Cue 9 At end of Scene (page 42)
   Dim to BLACK-OUT
Cue 10 When RUNNING TABS are closed (page 42)
   Bring up lights

ACT II SCENE 4 Exterior
To open; Lighting as Act I, Scene 2
Cue 11 At end of Scene (page 43)
   Dim to BLACK-OUT

ACT II SCENE 5 Exterior
To open; Effect of sunlight
No cues

ACT III SCENE 1 Exterior
To open; Effect of morning sunshine
Cue 12 At the end of Scene (page 54)
   Dim to BLACK-OUT

ACT III SCENE 2 Exterior
To open; Effect of sunshine
Cue 13 At end of Scene (page 57)
   Dim to BLACK-OUT

ACT III SCENE 3 Exterior
To open; Evening effect
   Hanging lanterns lit
   Flood behind backcloth to illuminate windows in cloth, lit
   Floods inside door backings and windows of buildings R and L, lit
No cues

MADE AND PRINTED IN GREAT BRITAIN BY
LATIMER TREND & COMPANY LTD PLYMOUTH
MADE IN ENGLAND

www.ingramcontent.com/pod-product-compliance
Ingram Content Group UK Ltd.
Pitfield, Milton Keynes, MK11 3LW, UK
UKHW021846210426
5322IPUK00022B/498